Live...

A MODERN NOVELLA BY JF KRIZAN

ISBN-13: 978-1481173179

Dedication

This book is dedicated to
William Gaius Krizan (1913-2008)
and all my fellow alumni, friends and colleagues
who practice a values-driven style of business
while seeking balance in their lives.

Acknowledgements

If we are listening, we have choices, to consider or not, and if a certain path seems honorable, then we may act or not, but we will only know the Truth when our resolute action results in a greater good. Thank you for your significant contribution to the *Live* journey.

Domenic A. Narducci III
Dr. Dietrich Schaupp
Dawn Handschuh
George R. Cline
Gary C. Sain

Chapter Contents

Chapter 1

The Juxtaposition of Right and Wrong

Originally, this book was titled "Live, Love, Laugh & Be Happy: Applying Old-Fashioned Values to a Highly Competitive Business World." Not only was that a mouthful but it may have seemed inconceivable how the three elements: happiness, old-fashioned values and the business condition were all interrelated. Maybe it would have been understandable that increased happiness could be derived from embracing old-fashioned values but why would that be necessary in the workplace? And so the story begins.

If you were a male born in the United States in 1913, your life expectancy was 50.3 years, so a man who was born in that year and lived until age 95 had truly lived a long life by actuarial standards. But when my father was dying a few years ago at age 95, I still hoped that he could go on a little longer so I could continue to extract and absorb as much understanding from the man who seemed to have all the answers to living a balanced life. Nevertheless, through all those years together, and in our final one, I was truly grateful for the traditional values (some now say old-fashioned values) that he had imparted to me and grateful for the positive impact they had in my business and personal life.

It will be rather common for readers of *Live* to have already benefitted from such a kindred relationship; a values-driven succession from those who came before us. However, it is just as common that these same honorable values are not consistently applied in the world of business. Why? Some of the same loving fathers, mothers, sisters, brothers and best friends inexplicably coat-check their fundamental values at the office door and then proceed to ransack the organization without conscience. There is no logical reason why the business community should engender a lesser degree of moral judgment than any other facet of life.

Far too often, there is a tendency for managers to deviate from their instinctual values. They seem to adopt a moral indifference from the allure of short-term profits, absence of established company protocol, feeling of omnipotence or unrelenting board, stockholder, coworker or competitive pressure. More to the point, some managers are weaker in character than others and succumb. A consistent application of traditional values is not so easy in business, nor is it always popular, but it is necessary for sustainable success.

But what are traditional, or old-fashioned, values? Wouldn't they be different between nations, states, social groups, ethnic groups or religious groups? Yes, they could be different, but from the perspective of *Live,* "traditional" values will always refer to values that are basic to nearly all of humanity. At the very least, traditional values will always fall within the prevailing jurisprudence of the time and place.

Values that cannot be legislated, which are more like a moral code, are largely covered by the Golden Rule maxim. Readers should be familiar with it in one form or another as most of the world's major religions ascribe to some version of "treat others as you would expect them to treat you." I have always considered the equal exchange described in the Golden Rule as an expectation. Far beyond my simply wanting or hoping for the balanced outcome, I expect equal treatment from others, as do most people.

Inclusive of the prevailing law and the Golden Rule, it is also my expectation that all business transactions are made at "arms-length." Business intercourse that does not rise to the level requiring a signed legal document is always being conducted by parties on an equal footing, independent of one another, even when interacting with coworkers. By conducting business based on this assumption, any agreements, disagreements or misunderstandings will be able to pass legal muster.

Finally, beyond the prerequisite adherence to law, reason and equality, traditional values include quintessential qualities of character including trust, responsibility, compassion, respect, leadership, ingenuity, benevolence and even forgiveness.

Live will also convey to the reader that businesses which promote traditional values will be more competitive in the world market and more sustainable than those which promote a divergent business philosophy. Just as it would have been unimaginable for the financial and market tactics of nineteenth-century, American robber baron industrialists to prevail through the twentieth century, it is equally unimaginable that inefficiency, pollution, corruption, depletion of natural resources and generally self-serving management can survive much longer in a highly competitive business world. "Sustainable" can mean business survival from one month, year, generation or century to the next, but sustainability should also mean business growth through adherence to the basic principles of environmental protection, human dignity and worker safety. Beyond the scope of the law, close adherence to these principles has been mostly voluntary; however, accountability and penalties are becoming increasingly necessary to constrain those who choose to exploit our natural and human resources.

Live illuminates specific lessons that can be learned from exemplars among us juxtaposed against the undesirable repercussions that follow a callous disregard for fundamental basic values. Several examples of unscrupulous business conduct in *Live* may seem laughable, inexcusable or deplorable, but the tragedy of these actions is that they were wholly unnecessary and avoidable. If business managers had simply taken a more values-based approach, they could have enhanced the opportunities for business success and sustainability. It should be noted that not all of the examples describe the unscrupulous activities of business managers; some scenarios focus on the importance of management preparedness, in body and mind. These do not evoke the same reader emotions as those which recount intentional unscrupulous behavior. Instead, the actions of the unwitting central characters are sad and disappointing because the results degrade sustainability, cause irreparable harm to coworkers or worse.

Understandably, it will not be productive to imitate the pernicious decision-making behavior of some people you may know or some of those who appear as examples in *Live*. However, we can benefit by witnessing or reading about the consequences of their actions, together with an understanding of what compels them. *Live* is an opportunity to reinforce the rationale behind some of the traditional values by which we already conduct ourselves and arouse those values that may lie dormant. Active, ingrained, wired or predetermined traditional values are part of our moral fabric as people.

It is an anomaly of the highest kind when some individuals who reach adulthood, know the difference between right and wrong and understand the potential consequences of their choices will still choose a destructive moral path that permeates every business decision and every action. Such was the anomaly of Bernie Madoff, founder and chairman of Bernard L. Madoff Investment Securities LLC (1960), who was sentenced in 2009 to one hundred fifty years in prison following a conviction related to his Ponzi scheme. He defrauded thousands of investors of millions of dollars in what is said to be the largest case of financial fraud in U.S. history.

Live is neither a book about corporate villains nor corporate heroes. There are many more examples of unremarkable people who represent anomalies of a lessor kind than those at the level of Bernie Madoff. Yet, they were all able to flourish within the system by means of a fallible conscience and permissive or unwary convention. There will be other examples of the "everyman" doing the right thing, all the time, at work and outside of work. Because they are the majority of people around us, their values most often go unheralded and hardly ever receive the credit deserved for the way they work and live.

Live is a story for everyone. The protagonist, an everyman born into the Greatest Generation, sought the life of a balanced man through his family, work and friends. During that journey, he never measured his success in any other way than his own quiet personal assessment of his love for family, the love that was returned to him and the bounty he reaped from touching others' lives. Through his actions and deeds, reassuring words and wit, he spread laughter and happiness to all who knew him. I always tried to apply his traditional values to my own life: in the early years, through college, when starting my own family and in business. Again, easier said than done; all of us can fall short of our intent, and I am no exception.

The man who once had hands the size of sledgehammers, olive-colored skin and a physique more like World Heavyweight Champion Sonny Liston was now skinny and frail, confined to a wheelchair and living in a twenty-four hour nursing facility a short distance from my home. I would soon discover that one of the most joyful periods of my life, on a par with my marriage and the birth of my three children, were my visits with him, spending an hour or two in his room, in the comfortable visitor's library or, on a warm and sunny day, sitting with him on the shaded patio.

Our conversations no longer resembled any of those from the prior fifty years in which he would admonish against The Great Depression, proudly recount his service during World War II or bellow out an old vaudeville theatrical song. Though the depth, and sometimes the accuracy, of his questions or responses in his final year were a shadow of his former consciousness, it was exhilarating to listen to him and watch the man as the words were slowly metered by his weakened body and mind.

I kept asking myself, *how or when did he get this old?* It seemed like it was just yesterday that he was teaching me many of life's lessons when I was a little kid in New York City, then as a teenager in New Jersey and later as a young adult starting my own family in Connecticut. Yes, I am much older now, too. At 60, I am now the age in undertaking *Live* that he was when I received my undergraduate degree in 1973 from Davis & Elkins College in Elkins, West Virginia. There is a certain irony, or perhaps appropriateness, in my now conveying what I encountered under his tutelage and how I applied his old-fashioned values to achieve business success.

While attending West Virginia University's Graduate School of Business in Morgantown, West Virginia (1974-1975), my Advanced Business Principles professor explained to me that "a more likely way of attaining an 'A' on course essays is to either take a very simple issue and make it seem extremely complex, or take a very complex issue and make it easy for anyone to understand." What follows in the ensuing chapters is neither! Instead, the subject matter is very simple, conveyed in very simple language.

I suppose I thought that he was old in 1973 when he was also 60, but maybe that was mostly due to his prominent white hair. Throughout my life, I have learned a lot from him, but one thing I know with absolute certainty, I do not know today all that he knew at my age. This was the artistry of him, through his life and until the end; I imagined that his calm nature, selflessness and insight were a result of some riddle that he had solved, some enigma of life or the way to live, love or find balance and harmony in one's everyday life. Relationships play a profound role in developing a unique values system for interacting with the world around us; they are the basic foundation that make us who we are and allow us to achieve results much greater than we thought possible.

Which one person in your life had a profound and positive influence on your values, what you sought to become and how you went about achieving your personal goals? Who will be the next person to impact your values-based development? Maybe it will be a relative, friend, neighbor, coworker or teacher, but it could be that you haven't even met that person yet. Don't be surprised if positive values are derived from fellow students while you are matriculating for a degree, certificate or simply attending a seminar!

Some years after graduation from Davis & Elkins College, an alumni panel group, organized as part of the school's Homecoming activities and representing a wide diversity of graduation years, was discussing their college experience when a question was posed to the panel: "Which professors were most inspiring to you?" As expected, the answers from the panel were polite and I was somewhat familiar with several of the named professors. Having a slightly different frame of mind, I was inspired to raise my hand during the Q&A period and let the small but attentive audience know how I felt. I suggested that while the panel's responses were understandable, my greatest inspiration at college came from fellow classmates like Blaine, Pete, George and Bill (who were all in the audience). They taught me, through my observations and interactions with them, that I was capable of achieving goals far beyond what I thought I could achieve. I wasn't sure if the audience understood my perspective but my account was very true in my case. Accomplishments in business, or life in general, will be a direct result of many other things beyond formal education.

I would be disingenuous if I did not acknowledge the positive influence I received from one of my professors at Davis & Elkins College, a gentleman who arrived the same year as I, to teach business and stimulate thought. Dr. Russell Studenmund had been an executive with Harcourt Brace Jovanovich, a major book publisher, and had decades of practical private sector work experience prior to our paths crossing. His pragmatic view of business rang true to me then and I am still highly respectful of others' practical experience today. Although he was not as polished a lecturer as some of the other professors, he was more adept in applying practical experience to the technical aspects of textbook academia. I related to that and it had meaning to me, delivered in his pleasant, familial manner. I'm sure there were a few other students who felt the same way.

Discovery 1

1) *Is there any plausible explanation why traditional values are not consistently applied in business?*

2) *Could you imagine yourself succumbing to moral indifference in the workplace?*

3) *Do you believe that people are born with intrinsic goodness?*

4) *Regardless of your current station in life, how do you teach and stimulate thought?*

Chapter 2

Ingenuity

My earliest recollections of him date back to when I was just a four-year-old. Back then, we lived in New York City, along with my mother and older brother (my sister would be born later), in an apartment complex called Stuyvesant Town, Lower East Side. It was a sprawling, multi-building, middle-class urban oasis with a network of playgrounds, walking paths and shade trees that created a harmonious patchwork of green grass, red bricks and gray asphalt within the chaotic appearance of the city beyond my reach.

His weekday routine probably resembled that of many of the city's apartment dwellers; he left early in the morning for an office job in Manhattan and came home late at night. Frequently, on his way home, he would stop to buy a small, plastic, model car kit. It was the type that had the pieces attached to a kind of disposable "plastic tree," requiring the builder to break them off and glue together according to the written instructions. I was far too young to be playing around with glue, let alone reading directions of any kind, but the greatest joy came from seeing the next morning how far he had proceeded in assembling the car for me. It was never finished the first night, and it was always done methodically, in multiple stages, perhaps to extend the joy I felt in seeing incremental progress over successive days.

This was typical of the care and detail that went into all of the fabulous things that he continuously created. He was rather clever and quite handy when working with wood, metal and just about everything else, as I would come to understand. Being too young to assist him in any tangible way, I just marveled at his ingenuity and the numerous creations in my early years.

I spent countless hours playing with the electric Lionel train set that he assembled onto his custom-built, small-town diorama creation. It was replete with a water tower, train station, milk-unloading platform and a pond, which used to be a hand mirror prior to his finding this splendid alternative use. The "grass" on this fantastical train town was some kind of fine-grained and dyed sawdust that he had sprinkled and glued onto the 4 by 6 foot surface. The resplendent lawn was crisscrossed by narrow, winding walking paths that were created from some leftover sand from our guppies' fish tank and glued in place.

The train town layout was securely hinged and fortified against the wall in my bedroom, directly adjacent to the side of my bed, and was only usable if it was carefully unhooked and lowered onto the bed. Because his creations were always well engineered, I never worried about an accidental release and collapse in the middle of the night while I slept. The Lionel #2037 Engine and the rest of the train equipment were always stored in a separate box under my bed and survive to this day. The train town eventually became age-obsolete, but you can be sure that its creator eventually found some other use for the wood in yet another one of his masterpieces.

Just as when building a model train set, care and detail in business planning should always be executed before your own creation is assembled, introduced and promoted, lest it become unhinged! The business success you achieve through ingenuity and creativity will not be solely based on your ability to skillfully work with your hands (unless you are a craftsman, doctor, artist or musician). Your own "train town" should be your frame of mind that's receptive to new ideas, your aptitude for envisaging concepts from nothing and your ability to continuously create. Imagine the opportunities afforded by conceptualizing a splendid alternative use for discarded items or by creating a greater good, either of your own accord or through collaboration with others.

Having spent a portion of my career in plastics and plastics processing equipment, I had a good view of the initial planning stages and launch of the eco-friendly plastic lumber industry in the early 1990's. It required the collaboration of many creative minds to resolve the cost, technical and marketing issues associated with manufacturing useful products from recycled plastic bottles. Through recycling, sorting and extruding plastic waste, forward-thinking companies were able to produce attractive and competitive home and commercial deck products.

Some of the most successful U.S. companies were rewarded by the collaboration of two or more creative thinkers and entrepreneurs, creating a splendid alternative use for existing products or services. EI DuPont de Nemours and Company's invention of low-coefficient-of-friction Teflon[®1] took a long while to reach a large-scale market. Being invented before World War II, its earliest applications were almost exclusively for the military. Some forty years after its invention, through the vision of Marion Trozzolo, an unrelated entrepreneur and founder of Laboratory Plasticware Fabricators, a non-stick Teflon[®] coating was first applied to frying pans in the United States, creating "The Happy Pan." We had one in our kitchen; it was a great product and an extraordinary market success.

A corresponding event occurred at the 3M Company, another international conglomerate and manufacturer, following its invention of a low-tack adhesive. After years of unsuccessfully searching for a use, a creative company colleague randomly crossed paths with the adhesive inventor at a seminar. Through their collaboration, a new consumer product was developed and marketed as Post-It-Notes[®2].

Many people I know make claim to thinking "outside the box" and like to wear it as a badge of honor. Yet there is no tangible evidence that any of them ever had a creative idea like starting a small in-home company, seeking a copyright or patent or discovering a faster-better-cheaper-safer way of doing anything! Having an outrageous idea may not place you in this infinitely small category of imaginative people; it may simply make you outrageous. Remember, whichever of these categories you may fall into, and whatever idea you may have, your original thought may not result in a successful conclusion unless you think it through. Consider the downside ramifications and analyze your creative idea from more than one perspective, even through collaboration, before announcing it to the world.

Your effective use of creativity is so important to the success of your company that it deserves more attention. The same goes for entrepreneurship, which can be exercised within the company for which you work, or in your own company, where you will assume all of the risk and reward. At times during the last few years, I was sometimes frustrated because my employer was asking me to create new business opportunities by building factories, improving profits, formulating new chemicals or inventing something, all without any apparent collaborators. When looking to my colleagues for creative synergy, it became evident that creativity and entrepreneurship were just not part of their nature.

All of my colleagues were specialists in their respective disciplines, whether it was customer service, IT, sales, marketing, engineering, planning or accounting. Collectively, we were already a harmonious patchwork of talents and personalities, but it was nearly impossible to draw them into a creative state of mind within the time constraints of the projects usually being considered.

I began to think that my having some degree of workplace creativity was unusual and that its conspicuous absence among those surrounding me was more the norm. I also believed that it was impossible to teach creative thinking or entrepreneurship, in much the same way that "you can't teach size to a football player within a week," a phrasal idiom that I picked up from my son. Maybe you have to be born with the knack? But, knowing that my own creations would be modest compared to the potentially unlimited creations of a free-thinking group, I made every effort to draw others outside of their comfort zone. I sought to have them join me inside the creative perimeter where change begins, a place where I was comfortable enough to offer a wide net if they strayed too close to the outer edge, where successful outcomes are no longer as predictable.

My effort to solicit creative responses from others was most consequential in the initial stages of a project to site and construct a chemicals plant for SATOCHI Chem America, Inc (SCAI), the U.S. chemicals division of the $15 billion Japanese conglomerate, C. SATOCHI Corp. As expected, the project was a more complex undertaking than I would approach alone and far more labyrinthine than the metals sintering production I had initiated some twenty-five years earlier at Wyckoff Alloys Corp (WAC), a small New Jersey metals converter and distributor I co-founded with Sal Damone (who you will read about shortly). Yet now, prodded by necessity and my encouragement, those in my group left their comfort zones one by one and rallied their quiescent abilities to make significant individual contributions to the new project. Although readily available, time constraints had not allowed any of us the luxury of enrolling in creative thinking classes, seminars, instruction and self-study through numerous books on the subject.

Perhaps the most practical method of awakening creativity in this project was through delegating areas of responsibility. With this particular project team, that alone was probably enough to arouse creative spirit, as the participants became fully engaged in body and mind from that point forward. Yes, additional encouragement to remain outside their comfort zone was occasionally necessary. I had to instruct one of the team members that he was no longer permitted to repeat the same ideas to the group when they had already been presented and vetted. In a similar fashion, when there were some (including myself) who hadn't sufficiently organized their thoughts prior to a meeting, I restricted project meetings with individual team members to fifteen minutes. This enforced a more efficient use of our time and we all became much more efficient in our interaction and decision making.

Sometimes I had to deploy the old tricks to conjure up different points of view and get us off center and moving forward. I recall being stuck a few times on some critical project decisions and simply got up from my seat at the conference table to take a seat on the other side. I frequently found that changing my physical perspective altered my creative perspective on a stubborn issue. At other times, I chose to change meeting venues entirely; whatever it took, I reasoned. Still, potent creative thinking and game-changing entrepreneurial thought are scarce commodities within business administration!

Consider how many small or even substantially sized family-owned businesses close or are sold after the founder's passion, creative thinking and entrepreneurship is genetically diluted in the second, third or fourth generations. Of course there are many other contributing factors in generational, family-owned business failures, like incomplete succession plans or sibling rivalry. However, survival partly hinges on the success of an aggressive pursuit of creative continuity. You may know some failed local, multi-generational, family-owned business that was exceptional at one time but simply could not survive beyond the founder's retirement.

The political environment in the United States had always been ancillary in starting new businesses, and the economic conditions had allowed small business to thrive, but today, there are other shifts which are also proving fatal to business. There are many examples of multi-generational businesses that are not able to sustain the founder's spirit. The U.S. Small Business Administration (SBA) reported in 2012 that only 30% of founder-generated businesses survive into the second generation under family ownership, 12% into the third generation and 3% into the fourth generation. The SBA also reported that more than 50% of small businesses do not survive past the first five years; so if you manage to hang on beyond that, you are doing better than most, and if you survive into the second generation, you are doing exceptionally well!

Within ten miles of me in Connecticut is an improbable, yet extraordinary, family-owned business which originated in 1797;

that's staying power! In their case, post-founding generations anticipated market needs with timely, well-conceived decisions, directing the company to supply market-appropriate goods and services, all the while remaining small and agile. In their two hundred plus years, the Waterbury, Connecticut-based business evolved from supplying sawmill products to metal stampings and zinc products. The Platt Brothers and Company, as they are called today, is still small, but few companies can trace their roots back to a time, five years earlier, than EI DuPont de Nemours and Company!

Also consider how many of these small, family-owned businesses overcame early obstacles, only to become floundering national companies with much bigger management problems. How many small, family-owned businesses sold their interests, only to watch their company become rationalized and relegated as a small division of a larger conglomerate? Yes, it is difficult—extremely difficult—to sustain the founder's creative advantage in an ever-changing world of governance, fashion, resources, competition and ill-conceived executive strategies.

Sometimes it takes a few years; sometimes it takes decades, or sometimes a century or more for the originality to degrade beyond recognition, then collapse. You may not be familiar with century-old niche companies like Hitchcock Chair Company (1818), known for its easily identifiable, stenciled furniture, and Seth Thomas Clock Company (1813), the producer of fine wall, mantel and floor clocks, because both are essentially gone! To illustrate how multi-generational companies can lose their way, I chose these two companies, not because they are particularly well known, but rather because they were founded in Connecticut, my home state and site of my family's original homestead, South Kent.

By virtue of the Hitchcock plant originating in Riverton, Connecticut, and being a mass-producer of chairs and furniture on and off since its founding in the early nineteenth century, you can frequently see one of their decorative, history-rich, vintage pieces at auctions and flea markets throughout Connecticut. I bought a pre-owned, well-decorated Hitchcock side table a few years ago; it represents a classic style to this day. The founder, Lambert Hitchcock, achieved early success, in part from the time and cost savings realized from stenciling furniture instead of hand painting decorations. Before his death in 1852, the creative founder sold his interest to his brothers-in-law. The company eventually closed. Lambert Hitchcock would never know that the company he originally founded was serendipitously rediscovered and reopened in the second half of the twentieth century, only to close again in the early years of the next century. The Hitchcock® brand has not disappeared completely; the rights were purchased by entrepreneurs Rick Swenson and Gary Hath in 2010.

Just before the announced 1982 relocation of Seth Thomas Clock Company's manufacturing plant from Thomaston, Connecticut to Norcross, Georgia, my last surviving grandparent, Susie Bereghazy, then in her eighties, gave each of her grandchildren $2,000 to purchase a new Seth Thomas grandfather clock as a planned remembrance of her; and we did. As a full-line clock manufacturer, founder Seth Thomas was an innovator, and early in his company's history he was able to smoothly transition from producing antiquated wood gears for his clocks to more effective metal ones. Upon the death of the talented Seth Thomas in 1859, his son, Aaron Thomas, took over the business. Since then, the company has bounced between several corporate owners and was held in receivership at some point more recently. Although Seth Thomas Clock Company is no longer producing clocks, the brand name, Seth Thomas®, is still in use by Park Lane Associates of Providence, Rhode Island.

Jimmy Buffet and Ernest Hemingway weren't the only ones who found Key West, Florida, an inspiring place to create; so did three entrepreneurs named Henry (Hap) Arnold, Carl Spaatz and John Jouett. They founded and headquartered Pan Am (1927) in Key West to facilitate the delivery of airmail between Key West and Havana, Cuba, along with a variety of other strategic plans they would execute early in the company's history. Their efforts resulted in Pan Am becoming, for a time, the largest U.S. airline carrier. Iconic corporate symbols of achievement like its unforgettable blue and white logo, futuristic terminal at New York's John F. Kennedy Airport and the landmark corporate office did not reveal the challenging years ahead.

Before its eventual demise (a bankruptcy in 1991), a myriad of events happened to Pan Am. Events that "happen" are sometimes just that, unpredictable. But consider how many events affecting a company's survival are both predictable and preventable! Certainly not all are, but many are regrettably self-inflicted wounds; such may be the case when we examine the actions of Pan Am executives after the founders' retirements.

The harmonious patchwork of the three founders' vision, creativity and entrepreneurship was followed by the regularity of dissonant executive management decisions: unrelated acquisitions, the purchase of overpriced National Airlines, disregard for competition from more nimble airlines and an inexplicable attachment to less fuel-efficient jets. Consider these ill-conceived executive actions in light of external challenges that lay beyond their control. Two notable spikes in fuel costs coinciding with the 1973 oil embargo and the first Iraq War, government deregulation, terrorism and the 1988 bombing of Pan Am Flight 103 over Lockerbie, Scotland all combined to bring about the perfect storm for Pan Am.

Another destructive corporate malady is the unrealistic view that executives sometimes have of themselves, their company and certainly, their industry. Collectively, "corporate self-importance" is the detached executive view of the intended benefit that comes from using the company's product or service; it is corporate narcissism at its worst!

The Pennsylvania Railroad (1846) succumbed as a result of the intoxicating executive perspective of self-importance. A lethal combination of perceived self-importance with ill-conceived mergers, government intervention, competition among other rail carriers and, most significantly, alternate forms of transportation, doomed them to failure. Once the largest rail traffic and revenue producer among U.S. rail carriers, the Pennsylvania Railroad no longer exists.

This point of corporate self-importance may be well worn, as I have had the fundamental concept presented to me several times during my own formal business education. The following may sound like the beginning of a joke, but it isn't, and it goes like this: "Not knowing the occupation of an executive that a man had just met at a charity benefit, he asked, 'What business are you in?' With a broad, proud smile on his face, the executive responded, 'The railroad business.' Another executive walked over to the men and was asked the same question, and he responded, 'The newspaper business.' Then along came the owner of a glass bottle manufacturing company, who responded, 'The bottle business.'"

Your ability to think of your company in a broader sense than that of the three executives may save it from bankruptcy someday. If these executives had replied, "transportation," "media" and "packaging," respectively, they might have stood a better chance of leading technical innovation instead of reacting to it and losing ground to faster-better-cheaper market alternatives. Perhaps the companies that employed our three executives would have been better served by executive management capable of fostering a culture of creative thinking and entrepreneurship when confronting the omnipresent market opportunities and threats.

In the case of the "bottle business," during the mid-seventies I was supplying a customer base of at least fifty U.S. bottle producers with nickel-silicon-boron brazing powder used to repair worn iron bottle molds. Practically all of these bottle producers are out of business today or have gone through numerous bankruptcy filings, as is the case of Anchor Glass Container Corporation. Only two or three of my original customers survived to the present day because they understood that they were in the "packaging business!" This knowledge better positioned them to focus on new product development to produce lighter weight and lower-cost plastic and flexible containers.

Later on, at the beginning of this new millennium, I collaborated with Louis Bertrand, an extraordinary paper engineer at Starwide Inc. Through our effort to perfect unique lower cost coating pigment for Starwide's coated paper mill, we hoped to provide magazine and publishing customers with an improvement over competitive products, and we did. At the same time, Starwide was entering into a merger with Horizon Industries, a Canadian-based pulp and paper company, to become HorizonStarwide Inc. This, I believe, would have made the combined company North America's largest newsprint producer. How was a merger of this type a good thing? It sounded like a bad idea to me considering that newsprint demand was declining due to a downturn in advertising and reduced newspaper readership. The internet was now providing a portion of the information that newspaper subscribers and readers had historically obtained, including news, retail promotions and classified ads. Newsprint economies of scale could only be achieved up to a certain point, beyond which overhead costs increased. Regardless, they merged in 2008, entered bankruptcy protection in 2009 and emerged from Chapter 11 bankruptcy protection in 2010, doing business as Woodland Consolidated Inc; a much smaller and more efficient company.

Still today, if you met executives of companies engaged in the business of exploring, drilling, refining, storing and transporting coal, gas and oil, they would likely tell you they are in the coal, gas and oil business, respectively. Instead, I would prefer they describe their industry as "a provider of energy that runs our factories and powers our consumer products," or simply "energy." By declaring energy as their organizational purpose instead of the other colloquial epithets, there is an implied call to action for broader executive strategies to seize unlimited opportunities. By continuing to define themselves as coal, gas and oilmen, the threats posed by depletion of our finite natural resources become more real. The competitive business environment is not very forgiving of those who do not fully understand the scope of their business.

Discovery 2

1) Can you really teach creative thinking and entrepreneurship, or are you born with those traits?

2) What other notable inventions, products or services were created and brought to market through the collaboration of two or more creative thinkers?

3) Can you name some family-owned businesses that did not grow substantially, or even survive past two generations?

4) Think about corporations whose executives did not fully understand the full scope of their business or their competition. Can you name some current corporations whose executives are guilty of self-importance? Alternatively, can you name some current companies whose executives have done a better job of defining themselves to the market?

Chapter 3

Trust and Responsibility

I did not understand it as a kid, but responsibility is a hallmark quality that is earned through trust, not simply bestowed or given away freely. When my sister arrived in 1957 and we needed more living space to spread out, there was a ten-year wait list for larger apartments in Stuyvesant Town. It didn't make sense for my parents to hold out for one because it was likely that one of my grandparents would be invited to live with us at a point when they would be unable to take care of themselves. Thus, our family packed up and moved to a cozy house with ample room in Ridgewood, a fine suburban town in northern New Jersey and an easy commute to New York City. Along with many of the neighborhood men, he caught the bus at the end of our small, oak-lined street, and off they all went every day to their jobs back in the city.

After living in the apartment all of my young life, our modest Cape Cod style home offered many new adventures, but the grander adventure was always found at my grandparents' home in South Kent, Connecticut. Grandpa Joe and Grandma Maggie had emigrated from Czechoslovakia in the early twentieth century, but by 1939, they had found their way to South Kent after residing in New York City. They both proudly became U.S. citizens and lived on their bucolic, twenty acre, non-working farm for the rest of their lives.

Since their passing in 1957, the homestead was passed on to our family. My maternal grandparents, Grandpa Joe and Grandma Susie, spent their summers there while the rest of their time was spent in Queens, New York City, their principal residence. They also emigrated from Czechoslovakia in the early twentieth century and became U.S. citizens. My family would frequently visit the farm in South Kent on weekends and spend the additional two or three weeks' annual vacation time that he had earned.

I was no more than six or seven then, when unknowingly, I had also earned some privileges of my own; and the adventures always got bigger on the farm! I would ride my Schwinn Spitfire bicycle down the country road to the South Kent General Store to buy a 5¢ Fudgesicle. I was always expanding my universe, kind of like a six-year-old Christopher Columbus. I also did a heck of a lot of fishing in Hatch Pond across the road from the farm, catching mostly crappies and bullheads.

The adventure took on even grander proportions during the next couple of years when my brother and I helped out at Boats for Rent, the Hatch Pond rowboat rental business. When Grandpa Joe was too busy or not feeling well enough to walk down to the pond after the arrival of an eager customer, we were free to rent any of the seven handmade redwood rowboats. We proudly collected the $2.00 daily fee, and even better, we got to split the money.

But there were other grand adventures surpassing even that. As soon as he taught me to care for, load and shoot grandpa's well-worn, 22-caliber rifle, my target practice on any piece of scrap tin in the field was now redirected toward the uninvited, zucchini-munching woodchucks in the acre-sized garden to the south of the house. They were always hard to see under the high canopy of the lush garden produce, especially from my distant vantage point by the house. Even when I suspected their presence and would quietly approach with the rifle loaded, they would always be alert and either remain quietly unseen undercover until the danger had passed or quickly scamper away through the pre-set, steel trap obstacle course that had been laid for their capture. More often than not, they escaped unharmed from this sharpshooter with the damage already done.

I know now that my parents always had a watchful eye over me, as they should have. The process was simple: as I learned, they trusted. As I earned responsibility, they let more rope out for me to develop. Then came more responsibility and more trust I would expect. Notwithstanding, there was always a transparent tether to the trust; the length of that line commensurate to my earned level of responsibility. I never took that trust for granted and hardly anything was ever handed to us kids except opportunity. All this took place before I was eleven years old.

The reason that I go on about these adventures is to make the point that both my parents instilled their core values of trust and responsibility in me at a very early age, earning me the privilege to experience all of the wonderful things I've just described. To this day I believe that I have maintained a fully commensurate sense of responsibility; to family, work and friends, so their lesson stuck.

I am truly grateful for the trust and responsibility that I was allowed to earn over time. Yet, quite a few employees don't understand the simple sequential relationship between earning trust, subsequent responsibility and privileges. They may fervently believe they have earned an annual wage increase and expect it will be forthcoming. Or, they may feel entitled to the next promotion within their department, or even beyond that, I suppose. To me, it was always a very illogical employee assumption that wage increases are somehow independent of the employee's productivity, corporate earnings or even cost-of-living changes. Thus, it follows that there should not be any employee entitlement to filling a vacancy for higher level or lateral jobs based on years employed or gender alone. Even though it exists, there should not be any "next-in-line" promotion policy; being qualified should be the primary criteria.

Employees who allow themselves to be consumed by their ire from being passed over for promotions can significantly contribute to disruptions in organization productivity. I've been passed over for promotions but I never let it bother me beyond a day or two, and I always made an effort to understand the reasoning behind the company's decision.

My employment as assistant marketing manager at NICO Metals Inc, a small New Jersey metals foundry, was the result of discovering an inconspicuous 2 by 2 inch advertisement in a local newspaper, interviewing four times, competing against ninety applicants and finally accepting a negotiated offer. Frankly, with that much competition, I felt lucky to get the job! Two years later, I heard directly from Sonia Gerber in the Customer Service Department that she resented being passed over for that newly created job: the same one that I had competed for with ninety others, the same demanding review process which ultimately discarded applicants with only a bachelor's degree and the same one which sought candidates with a high aptitude for creative entrepreneurship to revitalize the company's sales and marketing program. For the two years leading up to Sonia's bizarre disclosure, I always considered her lazy, rude and inarticulate. She was always first to proclaim, when there was an additional task to be carried out, "That's not my job!"

When I politely reminded her of the minimum qualifications for assistant marketing manager, she reaffirmed my opinion when she informed me that "if I had gotten the promotion, instead of the company hiring you from the outside, I would be more interested in helping the company." Even though I was only in my mid-twenties, I had sufficient composure to brush aside her overt dissatisfaction with the company and me. Three months after her unsolicited disclosure, she resigned, never having changed her attitude. Although she did not report to me directly, for the benefit of the company, I was so glad to see her go!

About twenty-five years later, while working for SCAI, I was given a sales department to manage. Although it generated significant revenue, it was disproportionate in terms of manpower. There were only five of us, so there was a lot of daily interaction. One of the department members, Ana Dubcek, was responsible for import and export logistics. She had worked for the company for more than twenty years since graduating from high school and was still basically at the same job performing the same daily tasks as the day she started. Like my disgruntled coworker, Sonia, from decades before, the characteristics between the two were incredibly similar. When requested to perform any routine task, Ana would frequently return a blank stare, as if everything was a bother.

Even before inheriting responsibility for the department, it was quite common to see her in her cubicle, with her head on the desk, anytime during the day. *What was management thinking to stand for this?* I wondered. Ironically, Ana's boss would often ask me if I thought Ana was "dour," as a simple observation, not as a manager seeking to resolve the problem. Anyway, who uses the word "dour" and expects understanding?" But since I was the new manager, the first time I saw her sleeping at her desk, I asked, "What are you doing?" She informed me that she was taking her lunch hour and then went on to explain she had to work through her regular lunch hour to finish a transaction and was subsequently taking her lunch hour from two to three o'clock.

Knowing that this irreverent desk-napping could easily become a contagious morale problem or point of intra-department ridicule, I made a decision. I committed to invest a small part of the department budget to try to rehabilitate this unmotivated employee by providing her with training in the areas of self-awareness and motivation. This was to be my first and last remedial strategy with Ms. Dubcek because it seemed to be more immediately advantageous than firing this marginal employee and training a replacement.

The timing worked out well for us to co-author her annual Management by Objectives (MBO) program to include a company-paid, three-day seminar with Tony Robbins, the world-renowned motivational speaker on peak performance. After attending the seminar, her return to work was triumphant! However, within two weeks she lapsed back into her late-afternoon naps! Fortuitously, within a month she asked for five consecutive weeks' summer vacation, which I refused, as did the entire executive committee from whom I sought a second opinion. This prompted her to leave the company. I am not really certain why she invested more than twenty years of her career and life at this job and company unless it was only about the paycheck.

Ms. Gerber and Ms. Dubcek were two of many employees who challenged the minimum company expectations. Neither of them ever came close to earning anything: hardly the paychecks that they cashed, and certainly not trust or responsibility. Absolutely no manager, myself included, would ever consider giving them a promotion.

Analyzing this more closely, both of these employees had to know that they were underachievers, but they also seemed to believe that they were entitled to a lifetime job, unrelated to their performance. In the case of the first employee, Gerber, there wasn't any company-established MBO program at NICO; I don't even think there were job descriptions or annual reviews for any of us. But, she did virtually nothing to initiate a career-advancement discussion with her supervisor, who was thankfully not me.

You may not want to try this, but during my second job interview at NICO, the hiring manager and VP of Marketing Sal Damone, asked, "If hired, where do you expect to see yourself after five years with the company?" Without hesitation, I replied, "I will probably have your job," to which I quickly added, "and you will probably be president." Irrespective of my premature awkward phrasing, you must always take control of your own career advancement. Don't depend on your supervisor to babysit your career and definitely don't keep your career goals locked up inside you, just simmering.

As I mentioned earlier, the second employee, Ms. Dubcek, was already working under an elaborate MBO program at SCAI, but she only fulfilled the most elementary components—those that basically required her to show up for work. All of the important core objectives most aligned with the company goals were never met. While they can't resolve all employee misconceptions, a degree of effectiveness can usually be achieved through well-structured company job descriptions, objectives, accountability and honest reviews. I do not believe that either of these employees viewed their job as a career, but for others, more is required to earn trust and responsibility.

Still, if certain employees were not complaining about the nominal annual raise they received or about others who had been promoted ahead of them, they might be directing their angst toward their supervisor: how they knew more than him or her, how they already performed all of their supervisor's difficult work, or collectively, how they were overworked and underpaid!

Even though my attempt to rehabilitate Ms. Dubcek with the Tony Robbins seminar failed, it is very important for every employee, at any level, to seek continuous education through seminars, certificate programs or even the next level of college education. Not only will this allow you to perform your position responsibilities more effectively and keep you current with changes to best practice, but this will demonstrate to management, or potential employers, that you are doing all that you can to achieve peak personal performance. Company-sponsored tuition reimbursement is a substantial perk and should be acted upon if made available.

Whether you are self-employed or working for a company, you have a real opportunity to experience adventures that are not available to most other people. Besides being a source of income, a place to go every day or some activity in which to participate, contribute or belong, your job could very well be the ride of your life, an enormous personal and career growth opportunity. I frequently brought about some of my own growth opportunities through departments that I created and organizations that I founded or co-founded; but that degree of entrepreneurship is not even required to realize ancillary opportunities.

When I was initially pursuing my career in specialty alloys and chemicals, I did not consider that my work would result in regular collaborative missions to the UK, Germany, China, India, Korea and the Czech Republic, to name a few. My universe expanded early in my career, and rapidly; before turning 30 years old, I was travelling to the UK to discuss high performance alloys with the staff of Rolls-Royce, Jet Engine Division. At other times, I was taking appointments at the Dusseldorf Trade Fair.

Domestically, I was meeting with engineers employed by the German-owned plastics processing equipment manufacturer, Austerlitz/Bach Corporation, or meeting representatives of mining equipment manufacturer Union Carbide- Linde Division to help resolve some of their extreme wear problems. Through my work with Linde, I was fortunate to witness our successful drill bit tip trials at some extremely inhospitable open pit taconite mines in Minnesota. I can't tell you how many times I was asked if I was a metallurgist. I am not, but to respond to the question I replied, "No, but I am a very, very good guesser." This seemed to appease most and get a laugh at the same time.

With regular promotions came privileges, like more international business travel. Less important to me, I gained access to the executive dining room, which in the case of Tomlinson, Olin & Douglas Inc (TOD), a major national specialty chemicals distributor, was a restored Pullman Company dining car. Of course there were the occasional golf invitations, which I never really enjoyed as much as other colleagues, but I still considered them perfunctory.

But far greater than the thrill and rewards gained from international business travel or the other perks was the sustained gift of new friendships at home and abroad: Stewart Cox from the UK, Gavin, Tong and Ms. Zhong from China, DW Kim in Korea, Yamamoto and Hashimoto in Japan and Madhav from India. They would become my first trusted pathfinders as I entered their business cultures.

As trusting as I was in these colleagues, there were others I encountered through work who were more like the previously described zucchini-munching woodchucks. I could never really see what they were doing from a distance. I felt that the employers for whom we worked had controls and fences to keep them from doing damage, but I never really knew how much damage was being done until it was done and they were gone. I worked with several of this kind in my career. They were usually found in the most senior management positions, typically held stock ownership or options, were very clever and were often well-educated. One disarming quality they all shared, however, was a stellar work history. To call them corporate raiders would not be as inclusive as I would like to categorize them. They are not always found in Fortune 500, publically-traded companies, but they flourish wherever the crop is ripe for picking.

I found myself in one situation where I had been lobbying, for five years, for my turn in stock ownership at TOD, an employee-owned stock company. Nobody cared to listen to my legitimate request, regardless of the recognized achievements within the company and my related promotions. The Board of Directors was not willing to create additional stock nor was any current stockholder willing to sell stock to others to take profits. Instead, they were all waiting for what I anticipated: the sale of the entire company to a foreign conglomerate. When, not if, that happened, the stock transactions exchanged internally for a few thousand dollars and promissory notes would be worth millions. For perspective, TOD had annual sales revenue of approximately $400 million, had substantial inventory and owned the spacious New Jersey headquarters/warehouse facility it occupied as well as the sprawling surrounding property.

I took my case to the President, Mr. Minter, a man I would describe as disarming and visibly self-serving. At our brief meeting, just between the two of us, he was polite, but in an evasive strategy spent most of the time looking out his corner window, avoiding all eye contact with me. I realized that Mr. Minter had no intention of even discussing the subject of stock ownership. In one of those magical moments when you say exactly the right thing at the right time and don't need to think about what you should have said after five minutes or the next day, I asserted,

"That's the problem; you would have me believe that the solution lies beyond your office walls. Indeed, it does not; the solution is right here." He redirected his gaze from the out-of-doors toward me, but his silence was telling. I thanked him for his time, returned to my office, retrieved the resignation letter that I had prepared should the meeting outcome take the course that it did and submitted it to my boss's boss, our nonpartisan Executive Vice President Rydingswood.

The conventional protocol would have been to submit my resignation to my own boss, Vice President of Marketing Ben Smythe, but a major part of Ben's own career strategy was never to become involved in a controversial issue, and since stock ownership was certainly coveted and controversial, I spared him. All of this took place on a Thursday and the events that followed were wholly unexpected, to say the least.

On Friday, Finance Vice President Patricia Bergeron walked into my office and inquired, "Would you like to purchase some company stock?" Her question suggested that she had not communicated with Mr. Minter, so I asked if she was aware of my conversation with him just the day before, and she replied with a simple "Yes." Of course I was thinking to myself, *how amateurish can these two be?* I respectfully refused the offer, told her that I appreciated the gesture and informed her that I had, within the last twenty-four hours, simultaneously submitted my resignation and accepted another position. Further, my decision was irrevocable since I had already given my word to my new employer.

On Saturday, two days after my corner office meeting with Mr. Minter, he went to the hospital for some scheduled exploratory procedure. He died that day, in the hospital. Within a month of his passing, I learned that all of his accumulated stock was sold back to the company and then transferred to other select employees; of course I had left by then. As I anticipated, the entire company was sold within a couple of years to Vornamen AG, a German chemicals conglomerate. It made millionaires of stockholders like

TOD Regional Sales Manager Bobby Stockwell, despite their mediocrity. But before that happened, Patricia Bergeron became the new president and redefined the executive art of being self-serving by maximizing her own TOD stockholding leading up to the sale. After the sale, the company was never the same, although it still exists today. As for me, I started my new job at Esco White, Inc, a chemicals division of $4 billion Finnish conglomerate Esco Oy. And I never looked back!

Discovery 3

1) *What steps can you take to avoid non-productive office politics and criticism of others?*

2) *How can you earn the trust of your employer to achieve additional responsibility and privileges?*

3) *How can you create your own annual personal objectives for your work life, home life and academic life?*

4) *Past or present, who are some of the most publically recognizable, self-serving corporate executives?*

Chapter 4

Making Others Look Good

After living in New Jersey a short time, he quit working in New York City and took a job closer to our home to spend more time with his family instead of the lengthy time commuting with strangers. Although I never worked with him at his job, his former coworkers whom I met later in my life were always happy to speak in detail of his good nature, generosity in providing instruction or explanation to others, willingness to share his knowledge and predilection for making others look good.

He was exactly that way at home with his family; that was his nature and demeanor. He was never demanding, but he had an expectation that all of us would be cooperative with one another and that we would always strive to do the right thing. There weren't a lot of rules because they weren't necessary to keep all of us aligned with that philosophy. Most often, when there were multiple opinions of a path forward, a very informal process of family consensus-building occurred. He hardly ever insisted on a specific outcome because he trusted our ability to reach a mutually agreeable solution that was, overall, in the best interest of the family. He was never boastful and would prefer to make others look good rather than taking the credit himself. So it was very understandable to me why his co-workers described him as they did.

That kind of benevolent coworker is usually easy to identify. He's the real team player, harbors no hidden agenda, is willing to share his knowledge and is focused on the greater corporate good, as he should be. Regrettably, coworkers like this are not the norm. In my work experience there were many more miscreants seeking self-gratification through corporate posturing, by protecting an already fraudulent self-image and ultimately trying to hold onto their jobs through any means possible to ensure self-preservation.

There were a handful of such miscreants that became the scourge of my daily work life! They were stealthy, difficult to identify and truly rogues, by no means prepared to share or collaborate. They were obnoxious, secretive, arrogant, dismissive and disingenuous to the extent that they sought all of the credit and had no interest in sharing any of it, regardless of contribution. It's guaranteed that you will meet many rogue workers in your career, and sometimes they are actually promoted from operations to a staff position just to get them out of the way, thereby minimizing their potential damage to the company. Other rogues are blood-related to the company owner and are thereby provided with absolute immunity despite their outrageous behavior.

I always felt I had developed a moderate degree of business savvy since my first job as a ten-year-old delivering *The Bergen Record* newspaper. From all the years that followed, through my exposure to numerous companies, organizations and the personalities of those with whom I worked, I believed that I had things figured out fairly well. I was acutely aware of the business of business—how things really worked—but I wasn't able to anticipate some of the extremes to which rogues would go to enhance the way they are viewed by others.

I assumed many roles as the new assistant marketing manager at NICO, one of which was internal liaison with manufacturing. As the internal sales liaison, I would attend the daily early morning, cigarette smoke-choking production meetings to exchange information. The agenda always included new orders, production schedules, technical problems, delayed shipments and general problem solving. I always felt that the foundry business was not so much science as it was art, and many things could, and did, go wrong. For example, when we received orders for six custom cobalt or nickel alloy castings, we might make molds to cast ten of them to assure that six could pass inspection. Failing inspection was usually the result of porosity detected by final finishing in our machine shop, and how many we would have to cast was determined from records of our historical rejection rates.

So on a six-piece order where we produced ten castings, with the good fortune of all passing inspection, we would ship six to the customer. If we anticipated future orders from the same customer, the production manager could put the four remaining pieces in finished goods inventory, ready to ship against the next order. Alternatively, he could simply return the expensive cobalt or nickel alloy contained in the four unshipped castings to the raw materials inventory for immediate remelt; the exact path taken was never reported to sales on an inventory list! Generally, we produced what are called maintenance or replacement parts and relied on customers' repeat orders for most of our product sales.

When the sales department placed a production order, it would always include the customer's requested delivery. Very simple. But sometimes there was a rush order, maybe as a result of the customer forgetting to place the order or due to an unanticipated equipment breakdown. In the case of our airline customers, we might get an AOG order (Aircraft on Ground), which meant get it done fast and spare no expense!

One time, when I noted an AOG situation to Keith Savage, the production manager, he provided a seven-day lead time to ship; normally, the lead time was seven weeks. I had to inform the customer that their rush order could not be shipped earlier than seven days; they complained, but ultimately yielded to reality. You could imagine how ecstatic I was when I saw copies of the shipping manifest confirming our shipment two days after we received the order! I walked over to Keith's office to thank him for expediting the AOG order, but he bemusedly informed me that he already knew he had the parts in inventory from a prior order and simply shipped them without any extra effort. He told me that he kept the truth to himself because he "didn't want your department to get the credit." (He worked in the manufacturing department and I was in the sales and marketing department.)

There are rogues like this in practically every company; they are sneaky and are rarely challenged because their self-serving activities are infrequently exposed. But sometimes they are! NICO was a union shop, albeit a small one with a shop steward. The steward is a company employee first, but is elected as a representative to outside union leadership. As shop steward, Lou Benedetto was a significant rogue, and I was told that he would frequently stand up on a 55-gallon drum in the middle of the shop floor, yell out some unsubstantiated complaint against management and then order the union rank and file to walk out in shared protest.

His only motivation was to impress the local union leadership which could have handpicked him for a position within their organization. Now this all happened before I was hired, but I came to know Lou after he became our complacent scheduling manager. His promotion to that title, into management with salary and benefits, disqualified him from being shop steward any longer. The sole reason for his promotion was to contain him from constantly disrupting production. He continued to operate on his own, still rogue, without challenge or reprisal for as long as I worked there. It seems that Lou may have achieved his goal after all: a cushy job for life with an ironclad employment contract. He was untouchable!

You should now have an idea of the destructive effect of allowing these kinds of workers to permeate the workplace, especially in a small company like NICO. Engineering a corporate culture is ultimately the responsibility of executive management. Unfortunately, in addition to the NICO rogues just mentioned, most of the other employees were underachievers; I already introduced you to Sonia Gerber. New hires at NICO (at least the ones with self-respect and a modicum of work ethic) left the company in short order because they understood that their efforts would not be rewarded or even recognized.

There certainly was no visible trust or respect among employees or any collaborative effort at NICO. Actually, executive ownership, through ill-conceived notions and schemes, promoted very aggressive in-fighting. For example, Sal Damone was hired as vice president of sales and marketing within a month of Tony Baldwin's hiring as vice president of manufacturing. Cruelly, the executive owners had informed both men that the intended plan was to promote the more effective vice president to president after a year.

The strategy was a complete failure from the beginning as that environment only bred contempt and self-promotion and worsened as the executive owners' plan became company-wide knowledge. By that time, the poison had spread throughout the company and became the new corporate culture. You now have a better understanding of what motivated Keith Savage to mislead the sales department. It was simple; his boss was Tony Baldwin, vice president of manufacturing! The company closed within a few years but not due to the devious behavior of Keith and Lou, or that of other coworkers described later in this book. The core reason for the "failure" will be discussed in *Live's* "Of Financial Matters."

Years later, while working at TOD, I was very pleased to learn that I would be replacing Porter Benjamin, one of the marketing managers planning on retiring. He had been an industry veteran and had already retired from PB Consolidated, a major chemical producer of titanium dioxide. Titanium dioxide is a white pigment used to impart opacity and whitening to a variety of products including paint, plastic, ink, paper, rubber and ink. Having worked for TOD about ten years, he was now probably in his mid to late seventies. *Big shoes to fill*, I thought, but I never worried about a challenge. Instead, what I experienced was a nightmare that lasted six months; it was a so-called "training program" intended to teach me the nuances of this critical, revenue-producing job.

My days were scheduled entirely by Porter, a rogue beyond proportion. Within a week, through his actions, he revealed himself to be a secretive, dismissive and self-absorbed employee who had no intention of sharing or passing along any files or knowledge of any kind. His main priority was to continue his established daily routine which included a two-hour cocktail lunch in between his morning and afternoon breaks. And he always tried to squeeze in a visit to his curling club down the street.

46

During my first week of training, he created the appearance that he knew what he was doing, but he couldn't keep up the charade any longer. After a month had passed, he would return from lunch, close the door and sometimes take a nap at his desk. How did I know? I couldn't have missed it because his executive office had been rearranged to accommodate my training program and an additional desk for me. I also discovered that he was telling other senior executives that the training was going a little slow but he was staying on top of things. When the president, Mr. Minter, asked me privately how it was going, I made a deliberate decision not to reveal the incompetence of my wayward mentor nor his miniscule contribution to the company.

Six months later, Porter was officially retired. He'd been given a generous severance package and a ceremonial going away party. Some of my peers at the company congratulated me for surviving the program with Porter. They told me that I demonstrated considerable tolerance for him and could never have survived six months of his nonsense! It's all true—the paltry effort that Porter made over the last ten years was all in the name of enhancing his image in front of senior executives.

Before moving on, I should warn you about one other kind of rogue. You will only find them in family-owned or -controlled businesses, and they can be present at any level of the organization. Ajeet Chemicals, a small but expanding national supplier of pigments and dyes, had many self-confident, productive family members contributing to the success of the company. But there was one guy who simply refused to follow any company protocol, because he was "the cousin," Rajesh Malik. He would with forethought and intent, conceal from the regional sales managers in the field, customer communications for them that were made directly to our headquarters. He most frequently positioned himself at our Midwest headquarters, grabbing customer phone calls and providing some degree of sales service, I suppose; but I could not be certain what he conveyed to our customers, nor was he ever directed to break from the established procedure to intercept these phone calls!

As a regional sales manager, I never would have guessed that the same customers with whom I was talking on a regular basis—trying to make appointments or provide test samples—were also talking to Rajesh Malik. More than the other rogue coworkers mentioned earlier, this guy was audacious and compelled to act by another dynamic—his strong compulsion to please his family, at the expense of everyone else. He was probably the sneakiest of all of my rogue examples; however, I usually discovered his questionable practices through his own confessions, just before I would have discovered them on my own.

He caused real damage to my sales program, although among the other dozen or so family members working at Ajeet Chemicals, he was a highly regarded company asset. In my eyes, he would have been unemployable anywhere else. On the occasion of a national sales meeting, his behavior was revealed to be so abhorrent and counter productive that I later asked Ajeet Malik, the supervisor that we shared, "Is he stupid?" I actually would have been somewhat sympathetic if that was his diagnosed condition, but instead, my supervisor replied, "He's not; he's just trying to help. Please be nice to him and I'll talk to him later." Since the two men were first cousins, what more did I really expect? Yes, I know, perhaps I should have been more tactful, but I was well beyond the limits of my patience with all of his self-serving shenanigans.

Ajeet Malik would also break from protocol, making customer appointments in sales regions without informing the managers having that responsibility. I was a bit embarrassed on several occasions when, as a relative newcomer to the company, I tried to get appointments with all of the prospects in my territory. After days of persistence, I was able to get through to one particular high-value prospect by phone, but I was very surprised to hear her suggest, "Why don't you just fly out next Monday when two of the other Ajeet Chemicals guys will be here for their appointment?" Of course, I was totally in the dark but recovered fast enough to simply agree that might be a good idea.

My job at Ajeet Chemicals went from being ridiculous to even more ridiculous, and I could no longer waste my time trying to figure out who liked whom, which coworkers I shouldn't say anything to and who was untouchable. Even the founder and chairman, Mr. Malik, had similar family-driven idiosyncrasies, such as his aversion to delegating, which in his case had to be excused; it had to be! I stayed as long as I had to and then left the company to be managed by the Maliks, in the way it had been managed since its founding.

Discovery 4

1) *"It is amazing what you can accomplish if you do not care who gets the credit" is a quote attributable to Harry S. Truman (1884-1972), 33rd President of the United States. We all have egos, but can you put yours aside if you are managing a group?*

2) *Under what circumstances would you promote a company agitator to diffuse or remedy a recurring problem?*

3) *You are an executive at Tomlinson, Olin & Douglas seeking to train a qualified replacement of a retiring manager. Knowing that the retiring manager is not qualified to develop or execute a training program, what would you do?*

4) *Think of three benefits from working in a family-owned business to counterbalance some potential weakness in their governance.*

Chapter 5

The Complete Executive

He was the kind of man who would lead by example. He wasn't any kind of hypocrite who might declare "Do what I say, not what I do." Instead, he was the subtle embodiment of both substance and style. It appeared to me that all our neighbors and his friends from New Jersey respected him, knew his self-imposed boundaries and found fun in some common interests, like wine making. Even our dog respected him; my favorite family dog, Red, constantly followed him around—all around—and I suppose that made him the leader of the pack, which he was. I have heard many anecdotes of his popularity among his former coworkers; there were people whom he had not seen for many years who actually hugged him when their paths inadvertently crossed once more.

Wherever we were, with whomever he was speaking, he was polite: at a gas station, in a department store (it was rare that he would go), in the dairy store or in the hardware store. He would speak to you as if you mattered, as if you were on his level, regardless of age, and he certainly would never discriminate against anyone. There were no off-color jokes of a sexual nature or anything directed against minorities or those less fortunate; he was compassionate and forgiving. There was a total absence of profanity and total restraint. I would have to think that he might have said something quite radical if he accidentally hit his finger with a hammer while creating a home project, or when the Doberman pinscher attacked him, but I never heard it. (We'll get into the Doberman in *Live*'s "Being of Sound Body and Mind.")

In my entire life, I only heard him raise his voice one time. His anger was directed at my grandfather, who was haranguing me over something he thought I had done. My rescuer came to me after being bombarded with a continuous rant expressed in all of the Czech and English curse words known to me. Even though I was reasonably certain of my innocence, at ten years old I was fairly defenseless, and his actions in that case were quite justifiable in coming to my aid. Within a few hours, the misunderstanding was cleared up and all was forgiven. I wish I could say that I have completely inherited his superior level of restraint, but I can't.

Style will frequently trump substance in boardrooms, executive meetings and at all levels of management. What exactly constitutes style? It's how well you carry yourself, how you speak, how you dress, how you groom yourself and an uncomparable wit that constitutes style. But style alone can be short-lived. If you land a job because of style, or if you're promoted for that reason alone, you will likely be remembered for the brand of your tailored suit rather than what fills it—thus the term, "empty suit." Substance, or core values, along with the depth of your knowledge, is likely to make you a more effective manager and leader; unfortunately, it's more frequently passed over for style.

For a few years I worked alongside Bob Connell, a technically expert product manager at TOD. Although he demonstrated substance to our appreciative customers and was considered a good guy by all of us inside and outside the company, he was consistently passed over for promotions because he failed to convey the new company image, so it was said. There was to be a new face of the company, a kind of style, according to the principal owners, including Mr. Minter and Mr. Rydingswood. Bob became weary of seeing his sizable contributions to the company overlooked. He took a calculated risk; you would be wise in exercising caution if you're considering replicating it.

There was an executive slot opening up at our company and Bob made it clear to the principal owners that if he was not going to be considered for that position, he would be leaving to accept a comparable executive position within Alcoa Corporation's alumina business. Fortunately, Bob Connell got the internal promotion, was extremely effective, as I knew he would be, and later went on to become president!

I only saw that risky strategic maneuver deployed one other time, at the same company, of all places. It was initiated by one of the empty suits, Vice President of Sales Thad Richards. He was all style, no substance, but in his case, his ultimatum to become the next president was resoundingly rebuffed by the principal owners. He was let go about a year later despite his originally being hired for style, which was felt to reflect the new face of the company.

It takes hard work to maintain your core values, or what I am calling substance. This is especially true when you are being out-voted, pressured or in jeopardy of losing your job as a result of your righteous position. The recent corporate era has had more than its share of failed leadership as documented in the mega executive failures at Enron Corporation (former CEO and Chairman Kenneth Lay's conviction was vacated due to his death prior to sentencing), Tyco International (former CEO and Chairman Dennis Kozlowski- convicted) and WorldCom (former CEO Bernard Ebbers- convicted). There have been laws, like the Sarbanes-Oxley Act of 2002 (also known as the "Public Company Accounting Reform and Investor Protection Act") that were enacted to protect stockholders, employees and the public from this breed of morally corrupt executives who are largely motivated by personal greed and a manipulative style. However, these laws only make it more difficult, though not impossible, for corporate executives to mislead their boards, auditors, Wall Street analysts and stockholders sufficiently to cause excessive financial damage and widespread misery.

Frequently, failed leaders started out as honorable people who then did very bad things—because they could—and because others in the organization encouraged or condoned it, or at the very least, looked the other way. When two or more aberrant executives begin to feed off of one another, an ordinarily adequate corporate culture can evolve into a culture of acceptance, though it is doomed to failure. In the 1987 film *Wall Street*, the character of Gordon Gekko, a Wall Street corporate raider played by Michael Douglas, proudly proclaimed, "Greed is … good," and lured others into acceptance.

Be proud of your core values. Let your coworkers know what you stand for, guard your self-imposed boundaries and keep your moral compass calibrated to a higher standard than the laws intended to protect us or permissive corporate cultures provide or promote. Then, always be prepared to defend your higher standard when criticized or under attack.

Unfortunately, unless you are the company owner or chief executive (whose actions and words can shape corporate values), your values may not be shared by others within your organization. When that happens, be prepared to take a strong stand, but realize that you may become disenfranchised, ridiculed, ostracized or even fired as a result. It is frequently impossible for you alone to change corporate culture, and while your company is conducting business without proper controls or generally accepted accounting practices and may be ignoring employee rights, you have to be prepared to leave if the principle that you are defending rises to a high level.

In most cases, I would like to believe that executive management seeks the high moral ground, particularly in the protection and defense of their employees. Take the continuing problem of sexual harassment in the workplace. Esco White had been proactive in remediating and eliminating sexual harassment by spending considerable money training about three hundred of their employees to that end. A consulting company specializing in this field was hired to train and review all key aspects of this widespread corporate problem. Esco White should be congratulated for their initiative, yet within months of the program's conclusion, they were investigating the newest reported claim of sexual harassment.

While attending their annual sales meeting in Savannah, Georgia, one of the old-timers, quickly and without warning, groped one of our sales professionals at a company-sponsored cocktail party preceding our awards dinner. I know all the details because I was in that small group of six or seven when the inappropriate behavior toward Ms. Brown occurred, right in front of us. We were just talking, about business I suppose, when John Beausoleil, our sixty-something insurance manager, groped Ms. Brown—not once, but twice, within a few seconds. Her protest after the first contact should have been enough for him to back off and apologize, but then he did it again!

As part of a company fact-finding investigation, those who saw what happened were interviewed individually by top management. Mr. Beausoleil was summarily fired (or "retired") and Ms. Brown sued Esco White, leaving the company soon afterwards. I have no idea of the terms of settlement, if any. So, good that Esco White initiated the training program, good that Mr. Beausoleil no longer worked at the company and good for Ms. Brown for defending her strong position! I learned later that Ms. Brown had also sued the company where she previously worked, again for sexual harassment. Still, good for her, because she's the only woman and coworker whom I know of in my thirty-five year career who ever filed a formal complaint. Think about that: the sole instance in a thirty-five year span. Sometimes it's the only option available for employees to affect change where change is necessary.

I was a middle-level manager at TOD where our two vice presidents, Thad Richards (Sales) and Ben Smythe (Marketing), would frequently be going at it over some difference of opinion outside my open office door. Unfortunately, I was usually the most immediate victim of their bickering because each of them occupied an office adjacent to mine. Screaming, profanity and behavior more typical of teenagers were not uncommon. By any standards, these men lacked a modicum of restraint, possessed zero leadership qualities and displayed little respect for the position taken by the other, or regard for the owners and the rest of us. Actually, their total disregard for professional courtesy proved to me that both of these men did not even respect themselves. Their ineffectiveness and low esteem for each other contributed to their discharge within a short time. Richards was let go, for other reasons too, which I previously described in this chapter. Smythe was "retired," even though he was only in his forties. Smythe's retirement cost the company a substantial golden parachute and Richards got virtually nothing; it's so ironic, because both of these men were hired to represent the new face of the company!

Regrettably, you will see this kind of bad behavior over and over again. This is not a psychology book, at least not overtly, so you may have to look elsewhere to find the root cause; maybe it is jealousy, fear, diffidence or even excessive testosterone. The latter reminds me of a very special circumstance that further illustrates some of my key points in this chapter on leadership including boundaries, respect and restraint.

I was no more than twenty-five years old and working at NICO when I was left in charge of a tradeshow booth and the company staff attending, mainly salesmen. Sal Damone, the marketing VP, had departed a day earlier, leaving me to manage the remaining day before the close of the show. It was no big deal, but I really wasn't expecting what came next. It was a high-performance materials show in Philadelphia with lots of engineers, scientists and graduate students swarming about the booths looking for solutions to their emerging technology. We had about five salesmen talking to customers and prospects while staffing the booth, but if they were not directly engaged in an information exchange, their job was to step into the aisle and draw seemingly uninterested attendees into our booth for a more detailed company presentation.

Here's part of the backstory. Our salespeople were probably in their forties and fifties, probably not degreed professionals, and not likely professionals of any kind, as I'll explain shortly. It was practically common knowledge that two of our salesmen at the show, Mac Delbart and Michael Emmanuel, were competing for the affection of Deidre, the attractive, twenty-something, single woman recently hired as our receptionist. We all knew what was going on between these two guys; I knew it and everyone at the company knew it, but I'm not sure if their wives knew it.

Back to the tradeshow floor. I saw these two lusty rivals pushing each other while exchanging heated words in the aisle, but I couldn't tell what they were saying from where I was positioned within the booth. Sometimes, you'd just prefer not to be in charge, but nevertheless, I rushed over, wedged myself between them, and as they were taking off their sport coats to duke it out on the tradeshow floor, I gave them something they sorely needed: sound advice. I calmly explained, "I could not care less what you do to each other. Knock yourselves out if you want, but you're not going to embarrass me or your company on this floor as long as I'm here, so take it outside now or let's get back to work." Of course, I was accused of overreacting to the situation as both rivals quickly composed themselves, straightened their ties and got back to work. I really felt like I dodged a bullet there.

Leading by example can be a very effective tool in improving company morale and motivating others. If enough people see what you are trying to accomplish over a period of time, even the most sedentary employees or organization members should eventually climb aboard. It should be such a simple concept and one that is easy to execute, given the volition and abilities of the leader. But I find it practically a cliché now and hardly ever seen in the business world. Considering the extent of my interaction with hundreds of managers and executives in companies where I worked and at hundreds of supplier and service provider organizations, the roughly one thousand customers or client employees with whom I've done business, the dozens of board and commission members and several dozen more I've rubbed shoulders with through several political campaigns, you might expect it would be easy for me to conjure up executives who demonstrated this type of leadership. Not so! It would have been easier for me to identify this kind of leader had I done an internet search for "most admired corporate executives," or something like that, and picked the top one or two individuals who led by example. By conducting that search, I probably would have gotten over-exaggerated leader choices in the thousands, from multiple arenas: business, politics, medicine, sports, armed services, religion and academia.

But the targets of my own search are mostly real people with whom I've worked. I've witnessed firsthand the benefits that arose from the results they achieved in the organization. I have seen any number of factory foremen who made a point to always show others how to properly perform a task; I've also observed mid-level managers who frequently did the work of their subordinates to ensure that it was done correctly. They may have led by example, but they are really examples of training methods and incompetence, respectively. It hurts the company when managers do not or will not trust subordinates to do the jobs for which they were hired. Those managers who lack the ability to delegate are micromanaging to the extent that they are either doing the work their staff was paid to do or unnecessarily redoing it, doubling the cost.

The real quandary in presenting examples of managers mastering this type of leadership —leading by example—comes from having to penalize many of the candidates for their inherent weaknesses in other significant areas of professional performance and yes, their personal lives. I have seen those that led by example but I had to give them an "F" in other areas of their performance and character that related to their values, ethics and judgment. Sorry, but I am not one of those observers who can completely excuse some repugnant behavior simply because of an otherwise stellar lifetime body of work. I seek the well-rounded executive package for my nominations, where substantial digressions are neither condoned nor excused.

If anybody believes that I am being overly critical, take the case of NICO President Robert (Tommy) Tomalinski. He was a leader by example, but could hardly be put on a pedestal. You never knew what to expect from him. He could lapse into poor judgment at just about any time. He would, for example, invite and allow Deidre, the receptionist I introduced you to earlier, to sit on his lap through most of our company's Christmas parties in the late seventies. He frequently enjoyed his liquid lunches while the rest of us ate at his table. This kind of erratic behavior frequently gave rise to hushed employee conversations debating his fitness.

I interacted with many other leaders showing exemplary traits, but most also had specific personality flaws that effectively erased their names from my distinguished list of most well-rounded executives. Even Thad Richards, vice president at TOD, could go from magnificent to madcap within minutes; that's really the best way to describe him. Thad would impress and then shock coworkers and customers alike with his rhetoric or bad behavior moments later. Sadly, he was well known for inappropriate sexual conversation. When directed to the women in the office, It's something that I considered sexual harassment. And really, the rest of us didn't want to hear it, either.

Years ago I received a phone call from the wife of Sal Damone. After NICO, Sal and I became business partners of sorts in WAC. Once our office on the East Coast was up and running, Sal pushed to open another office on the West Coast and relocated his family to California to open it.

I visited him the week prior to the fateful phone call. It was typical of the periodic face-to-face communication required while running a business with offices on each coast. Mrs. Damone had called me to ask if I visited with a girl I knew from college during my California trip. It only took an instant for me to understand what the real issue was. Regretfully, I had to tell Mrs. Damone, "I'm so sorry. I have no friends living in California. I'm so sorry to have to tell you that." Although we all knew that Sal Damone was a creative, well-educated and generous man, we also knew that he had a drinking problem, a womanizing problem and was not forthcoming in a lot of situations. Obviously distraught, Mrs. Damone went on to briefly explain that she discovered that Sal spent the night with another woman. And as we now knew, he unilaterally and deviously tried to involve me in his moral failure. Later, I had very direct words with Sal about his inflammatory actions, which became a considerable factor in my determination that the two of us could no longer be business partners.

I have to mention Thomas McFee, former president and CEO of automotive and avionics systems producer Dextronic Corporation, not because I knew him, but because I was working nearby their Teterboro, New Jersey, plant in the mid-1970's. At the time, the radio and newspapers regularly reported on his corporate success, and something else. It seemed that the media could never report on his innovations in human resource management and unparalleled business acumen in achieving profitability without mentioning his alleged office romance with another overachiever, Margaret Hildebrand. Despite the Dextronic board's approval of McFee's appointment of thirty-year-old Ms. Hildebrand to executive assistant to the CEO and then to vice president of strategic planning, the media buzz was incessant. Unfortunately, the qualified Ms. Hildebrand resigned in 1980, citing the unfounded rumors surrounding her relationship with Mr. McFee as the reason she could no longer perform her duties. They married in 1982, which somewhat corroborated what was being reported. Afterwards, they both went on to pursue highly successful careers in business and philanthropy. Mr. McFee would certainly have been on my list of most well-rounded executives if it had not been for his inability to quell the negative media frenzy, one way or another.

I concede that we all have flaws and weaknesses. Put another way, "All of us are perfectly imperfect," including business people. However, I am very fortunate to have worked with a few who have distinguished themselves above others through their overall leadership abilities and their faithfulness to the fundamental precepts of values, ethics and good judgment. Each of these three managers was very different from one another, yet they were all effective in inspiring others to work for a common cause under their leadership. My short list of distinguished leaders includes Mr. Ackerman at John Ackerman Painting, for his trust in all who worked for him; Roman Evdo at TOD, who was indeed a gracious man; and Frank Perilli, the vigilant, aging co-owner at Gene's Beer Garden. Through his words and actions, Frank captured the essence of his leadership during one of Gene's famous summertime free beer promotional events. When it was 90 degrees inside and the place was packed, when it was only the two of us frantically working side-by-side to keep up with customer orders, Frank exclaimed to me, "If I pass out [from exhaustion], just throw some cold water on me and pull me to my feet."

Frank's comment may indeed sound melodramatic, but it was his kind of leadership, the kind of thing John Wayne would have said if it were a movie! You will learn more about my personal experience with Mr. Ackerman, Roman Evdo and Frank Perilli in *Live*'s "Few Things are Accomplished Alone."

Everyone can benefit from a mentor. Pick someone with substance, expertise and leadership quantities. By the end of this book, you should feel that you have been provided with suggestions for identifying a qualified mentor. That is not to say that in my own career I have selected my mentors properly or even objectively. Through most of my early career I made poor mentor choices because I was influenced more by style than substance, and the mentors I chose turned out to be something quite different than what I initially perceived them to be.

For example, I believed that the dapper Jay Ellsworth, one of the principals at the holding company owning NICO, was the consummate professional sales executive, a deal maker and a strategist supreme. His obvious persuasive qualities and charm made him a millionaire; sounds good to me, I thought. The escapades of Mac and Michael, the two sales guys who were about to come to blows over Deidre, our receptionist, have already been documented but I had no idea that my new mentor was also competing for her!

Typically, I would meet a few of my coworkers for Friday Happy Hour at Caesars III in Teterboro, New Jersey. Caesars was a very small, quiet, upscale cocktail lounge with few patrons. My group always sat at the bar, but the tables in the dimly lit dining area were sometimes occupied by only a few others unknown to me. I'm not sure how Caesars made their money, but I think I figured it out years later when I heard a prison interview with mob enforcer Richard "The Iceman" Kuklinski. During the interview, he scoffed at the unreported disappearance of a body he claimed to have stuffed in a garbage can near Harry's Corner, across Route 46 from Caesars. Kuklinski was so bemused by the lack of any media coverage that he also claimed to have gone to Harry's for breakfast a couple of days later to check and see if the body was still there. (It wasn't.) Kuklinski claimed to have murdered over one hundred people during his mob career and was said to be a regular breakfast patron at Harry's. Without knowing anything about that at the time, I also frequented Harry's, but at lunch, for their famous sausage and egg sandwich. But I really liked Caesars because it was close to work, quiet and very private.

During one such Happy Hour rendezvous, only a short time after we all arrived, Mac Delmon conspicuously ordered a bottle of wine from the bar, to go. (Never do that if you care anything about the value of money since a package store will sell you the same bottle at one third the cost.) He proudly proclaimed that he was going home to a homemade pasta dinner with his family. But by Monday morning, I was already thinking that Mac would be fired! As it turned out, he didn't go directly home from Caesars, but went to Deidre's apartment instead, with bottle of wine in hand. When she opened the door for him, he was able to see my mentor, Jay Ellsworth, sitting on the couch and looking rather perturbed about the unannounced intrusion.

I was still a sucker for mentors with style, being partisan to their expensive suits, fedoras (nobody wears these business hats any longer), fitted Qiana^{R3} fiber shirts or their desirable suburban homes with swimming pools. I'm having a little fun with this, but I gave up seeking mentors a long time ago because they are just so scarce; the last one dates back twenty-five years ago! Alternatively, I found it better to objectively observe and consider the pronouncements and behavior of management before I sorted it all out to keep only the gems and discard all the bricks. When anyone provided me with even a single pearl of wisdom, I was grateful and saved it as a possible solution for a similar future encounter.

Here's a case in point. During one of our annual sales meeting dinners I was seated next to Ms. Aakko Mikkola, president of Esco White. She was an expatriate; a term I use to describe employment in a country other than your own, usually at the request of the employer. I knew that Ms. Mikkola was nearing the end of her assignment in the United States so I was happy to spend some time with her. Our conversation turned a bit philosophical and she made the point that "personal freedom can only be fulfilled through options and choices." Was she a mentor? No way, but she did give me a gem to keep! She was contrasting herself to other managers who she felt were constrained by few opportunities for personal or career growth, or for changing career paths. She concluded by saying "I feel privileged because I have options." I guess she meant what she said, because two weeks later Esco Oy announced that Ms. Mikkola would be leaving to take a high level, executive position with another company. Since that dinner, I have always kept my options open for business and personal growth.

Discovery 5

1) *Make a list of five people who are more substance and five others who are more style.*

2) *How can you ensure that you won't be tempted to cross your own self-imposed boundaries?*

3) *What have you done recently to lead by example?*

4) *What criteria have you used in picking a mentor?*

Chapter 6

Of Financial Matters

When he was a teenager living in New York City, The Great Depression threw this country into despair and financial ruin for many years. Beginning on October 29, 1929, he became an eyewitness to despondent investors who took their lives by hurtling their bodies from upper floor office windows. He saw soup lines occupied by former millionaires and others reduced to living in cardboard houses in Central Park. He would always wince when recalling how some unfortunate horses, once hitched to wagons for transporting goods within the city, were left unfed to die in the streets. He described how their bloated carcasses remained in the streets because there were limited city services to haul them away. The flies found a welcoming home to lay their eggs, which soon became flesh-eating maggots.

It is safe to say that nearly all Americans who survived The Great Depression saw the world in different terms for the rest of their lives. A predilection for fiscal responsibility, savings, risk aversion and living within their means were all a result of that dire experience.

My own family was no exception. Because it was not in our family budget, I remember pretty well the few times and places that we ate out in a restaurant. I never really thought about going out to eat because we always ate at home as a family, and the food was probably better, too. No, I'm sure that it was. But when the announcement came on a weekend evening that we were going out to eat, I could not have been happier. His favorite place to eat was a restaurant near our New Jersey home, Aunt Jemima's Pancake House on Route 17, one of the major shopping highways in Paramus. He would usually order the "Silver Dollar Pancakes," which were the diameter of silver dollars and would come piled high on your plate; that was one of my favorites, too.

We really didn't go to Aunt Jemima's, or any other restaurant, more than two or three times a year. Eventually, the restaurant was sued for illegally using Quaker Oats' famous registered brand name, Aunt Jemima.® The owners eventually changed the name, but it was never the same after that, and then they closed forever.

Because we didn't receive any kind of regular allowance as kids, his frugality taught me to pay my own way, as much as I was able, and save. Beginning with my first job delivering *The Bergen Record*, I saved my money, bought gold coins (true) and still have them to this day. He had taught me the fun of coin collecting by initially giving me some that he had saved in his dresser drawer: starter coins of U.S., European and Panamanian origin. I was thrilled when either of my parents would take me to the nearby Bergenfield Stamp & Coin to rummage for deals in their bargain bin.

The 1904 Double Eagle (a twenty dollar gold coin), which I bought before I was twelve, was one of my most prized possessions. I eventually incorporated it into a belt buckle which I wore occasionally when I needed to remember who I was and where I came from.

More than anything, I always enjoyed using my savings to buy birthday or Christmas gifts for my family. So, I started working at ten years old and have been working almost continuously ever since. Even while attending college, I would wash dishes in the cafeteria, sweep the gym floor and paint classrooms with other students at night, but we always managed to make it fun.

Those college jobs were a form of need-based financial aid and did not require any job interview, but when I prepared for an actual job interview later on, I was never able to collect enough information about my prospective employers. Today, it is far less complicated to research an organization on the internet and through other sources, but vital information may still be overlooked during due diligence. In my case, had I done more, I would have had additional valuable information that could have provided me with insight into the prospective employer's fiscal responsibility and sustainability. Had I been able to access this information, I would have likely changed at least a few employment decisions. Since it was not yet created, I did not have the advantage of the internet while I was going through the interview process in the mid-seventies with NICO Metals, nor was I able to obtain any financial information about HiTone Inc, a privately-owned, plastic color concentrate manufacturer in which I was interested in partnering on a new venture; both eventually closed.

I was so enthusiastic about meeting NICO Metal's hiring manager, Sal Damone, for the first interview, and then the second interview, that I didn't have the presence of mind or courage as a twenty-three-year-old to ask about the financial health of the company or its anticipated growth. It's unlikely that he could have provided me with financial results from this private, closely held company, but maybe he could have shed light on what the company was facing in the short term.

What I didn't know until I started working at NICO was that the production equipment was gravely worn, depreciated long ago, and that the main product's patent was due to expire in four years. Unfortunately, the manufacturing costs for its high-valued, patented, hard surfacing welding rod (PWA 694), used for jet engine repair, was never accurately calculated. It turned out that our PWA 694 was greatly undervalued and underpriced. To make matters worse, any gross profit earned from the product's sale was substantially reduced by a royalty paid to its two inventors, T. Nutting and F. Broward.

Typically, an invention created on company time, by salaried employees, is a company patent; that is, one that's owned by the company. But in this bizarre circumstance, the company allowed the patent to be placed in the inventors' names. Within two years of my being hired, we got a better handle on the costs and raised the price by 350%, to $280/lb. On the downside, we created significant animosity among our customers, made the inventors even wealthier and swung the door wide open to incentivize a competitor's emerging manufacturing technology.

Within a year after our dramatic price increase, this creative competitor commercialized a unique process that could produce a higher quality PWA 694 at half our cost. The owners of NICO made the deliberate decision not to invest in this new technology and not to obtain a license agreement to manufacture under their new process. Soon after, unable to remain competitive, the company's sales and profits tumbled. Seven years after Sal Damone hired me, NICO closed their doors forever. (I left after five years because I didn't want to be the last man out the door. Sal Damone left a year or two before me in a cost-cutting reorganization.) In the end, the owners sold the remaining high value, cobalt and nickel raw materials inventory and the highly desirable, commercially zoned land to make an enormous profit. Sixty former coworkers lost their jobs. The building was redeveloped by the new owners into business condominiums.

In *Live*'s "Making Others Look Good," I refrained from saying that the demise of NICO Metals was brought about by the bad behavior of a few employees. But now that you have just read about the final years and aftermath of NICO, I can explain what I didn't understand when I was hired. The closing of the company was actually predetermined some nine years earlier, when the second generation family-owned company was purchased by a small predatory venture capitalist group. The new owners knew the equipment was worn, that the lucrative patent was expiring, that prices could (and would) be raised, that the substantial metals inventory and future metals contracts would appreciate and that land values would rise. In its nine years of ownership, the VC group leveraged this asset to buy other distressed companies, drew salaries, took profits and paid off the miniscule promissory note with the former owner. The closing of the company was never a direct result of employee shortcomings; it was the result and execution of a preconceived plan, but with a huge price to the employees who remained loyal until the end.

In my career, I was financially hurt by business relationships with three privately-owned companies that did not have sufficient financial means to support the level of business they sought and did not choose to live within their means. I'm not talking about unscrupulous people or companies that did not pay me for the goods or services I provided or went belly-up because of general economic downturns. I'm referring to owners who simply did not assume fiscal responsibility. Due diligence is necessary; asking the hard questions when interviewing and seeking verification is also part of the process.

In any career, there are many business and personal opportunities that can be created or just simply come your way. At one point, while employed as a national account manager at Esco White, I was rather happy with my job. I was traveling throughout the Northeast with only a few overnight stays, selling to an educated clientele and promoting product technology, with which I was very familiar, to markets that I knew. When I wasn't visiting customers in my company-provided car, I was conducting business from a home office; working out of my home, which I found to be very convenient.

Unexpectedly one day, I received a phone call from Bud McFinn, a gentleman whom I had met through business a few years earlier. He told me that there were some people looking to start an organic pigments distribution company if they could find the right person to manage it. He mentioned that my name kept coming up among the investors. I wasted no time in conveying my lack of interest, although I appreciated being considered nonetheless. A couple of weeks passed and I received another telephone proposition from Bud; again, I declined. Regret over a lost opportunity sometimes plays on the mind, and it did with me. Would I regret not even discussing it? That night, I raised the subject over dinner at home. Then, having established the expected family moral support, I waited for the anticipated third telephone call from Bud. This time I responded, "Let's talk."

Or was my judgment being clouded by the delicious prospect of running my own company, funded from the deep pockets of others, and of course, with the expectation of personal financial gains beyond my current compensation? Was I trading a secure, stable business infrastructure, which I had called home for five years, for a cardboard house, without even weather-testing it or performing a minimum level of due diligence? This was a really tough decision.

My entrepreneurial nature compelled me to accept the challenge and the reasonable initial compensation offer that came with it. Thus we started Lumitech Inc, our private brand, organic pigment distribution business. Despite the huge amount of time and energy that I invested in that business venture, we ceased operations within three years. The financial funding necessary to weather the blips in a new startup was simply not there; in fact, it never was. We were incapable of covering our meager overhead as prices and profits plunged after our largest competitors retaliated when we grabbed market share.

Having started my career in the seventies, I have now been an eyewitness to five decades of corporate pillage. It's easiest for me to make this point by discussing the corporations that I have either worked for or with which I had direct contact. Even during the seventies, the annual material and accounting swag (money, goods or services stolen from a company by employees) in the United States, combined with other corporate malfeasance, was hurting our global competitive position and forcing cost reductions in essential departments.

At one time, I was responsible for approving expense reports at NICO Metals. I found myself in the very awkward position of having to ask one of our salesmen, Ron Baxter, for an explanation of a line item in his expense report. It was not a generally recognized description to me. He reported something like "Loan to Mac Delmon- $50.00." Knowing that I wasn't going to let go of this and after I told him he was responsible for loans to other salesmen, he unexpectedly admitted that it was payment for a hooker during their joint business trip to a Midwest city. Expense report approval: denied!

I came to believe a long time ago that misappropriations, theft and payola were systemic. It was said (mind you, it was never proven) that one of NICO's customers, Bethlehem Steel Corp, at one time the second largest steel producer in the nation and the largest shipbuilder, would only consume a portion of our welding rod shipments because a pre-calculated amount would pass through their warehouse and go directly to their scrap pile or into the nearby river. It was rumored that one of their purchasing agents was receiving graft payments on every shipment we made; thus, the more shipments we made, the more unearned income rumored to go to one of their purchasing managers. Customer status update: bankrupt!

I would never have actually believed that graft was so prevalent within our country until a few years later, when a prospective customer's quality control manager informed me that the newly established Lumitech would never receive product approval from him or his company unless we paid him a 1% commission. As Lumitech co-founder, I wrote a letter to the CEO of their very large parent company complaining about this illegal practice, without revealing the name of the offender. Within a few days, I got a frantic call from the president of the division where I had sought to have our products approved, asking me for all the details of my accusation. I agreed to meet with him but didn't plan on giving any further details than what was contained in my letter to the CEO. Instead, I suggested that he should conduct his own investigation and that my company would no longer seek to solicit business from them. Customer status update: bankrupt.

I could go on, but there is just one more common example of corporate pillage, in the category of corporate swag. For centuries, swag has been pieces of company property employees brought home. Even more recently, I don't think employees considered it stealing, and if you had broached the subject with any one of them they probably would have told you, "The company expects it and they just write it off." That is never an acceptable explanation from a corporate perspective. The cumulative financial loss dramatically increases when pilferage of company pencils, copy paper, postage, highlighters or any other kind of office supply products escalates. For example, one of the executives at a company where I worked partially paid for the construction of a substantially-sized house with purchase orders run through the company, right down to the imported, custom-made, front door hardware. Company status update: closed.

When discussing examples of companies picked clean from the inside, a business editor I spoke to suggested that there was an even greater destructive force besieging U.S. companies in the seventies. She was referring to foreign competition. It's no surprise to me that U.S. manufacturing began to erode in the seventies, a time when foreign competition became leaner, more competitive and invested in new equipment and technology. There were a lot of union workers employed by U.S. manufacturing in the seventies, even at Bethlehem Steel, where the powers that be collectively wondered how it was possible for Japan, for example, with virtually no natural resources, to produce steel I-beams, rails, plate, rod and wire, ship them across the ocean and price-compete with our iconic steel corporations.

Having given the editor's point of view some thought I maintained that the larger destructive impact to U.S. business came from within. Stolen laptops alone do not make my case, but when you combine that with the substantial economic damage from reductions in R&D budgets, creativity droughts and self-serving executives with their moral lapses and fundamentally poor decision-making, my case is made. I maintain that the villains in the story were not our competitors, domestic or foreign; rather, they were scattered among us and working beside us as they ate away at our weakening manufacturing technology and financial underpinnings.

Still, it seems impossible for me to rationalize the kind of corporate executive behavior that results in corporate pillage; it seems un-American! Maybe those reprobate corporate executives did not experience The Great Depression, never had to wash dishes to pay for college and always expected to dine at restaurants as children. But, if they did, and still pillaged, I am relatively certain that they lost their way during their rise in the corporate world and couldn't remember who they were and from where they had come. There are fewer and fewer Depression-era eyewitnesses and survivors alive today, but if the rest of us have learned anything from that debilitating period in U.S. history, we should have a better sense of what triggers can cause a reoccurrence and which corporate policies and strategies to avoid. There was a time when it appeared the massive manufacturing infrastructure on which many jobs rely could never be shaken; after all, we were the United States.

So how should these executives have weighed return on investment strategies against risk aversion and fiscal responsibility? Unscrupulous managers thrive in an environment where fiscal responsibility and control seemed nonexistent. Tony Baldwin, the vice president of manufacturing at NICO, actually fired our entire Quality Control Department, an essential operation and necessary cost of doing business as far as I was concerned. When asked for an explanation, I was simply told that "because we are under-achieving our short-term profit expectation, our customers will now be responsible for quality control." Note: his annual bonus was directly tied to profitability.

In a related maneuver, since Tony was still bent on chasing additional profits by cutting labor costs, he turned a blind eye to the shortcuts taken in the testing of the turbine valves that we produced for major steam turbine manufacturers like GE, Turbine Division. The faked quality control records were discovered during a GE quality audit, but they let our management off the hook with only a reprimand and we were ordered to dispose of $500,000 of our untested finished goods inventory. (In 2012 dollars, the value would be close to $5,000,000.) Was Tony Baldwin demonstrating fiscal responsibility by dramatically altering the risk vs. reward ratio? No!

I am going to walk a fine line here because throughout this book I will continue to discuss entrepreneurship, which is inherently risky but packed with the promise of great reward. However, there is a big difference when you are allowing high risk trades, transactions and investments for a public company compared to risking your own money or that of venture capital from private stakeholders in a startup.

In 2012 the world learned that a leading financial services firm, JP Morgan Chase, lost roughly $4.4 billion (and climbing) in what some analysts called "bad bets." After a litany of mea culpa's and a few extra mea maxima culpa's (my most grievous fault), President, Chairman and Chief Executive Officer Jaime Dimon was exonerated in the press and will continue to manage the company!

Discovery 6

1) If you cannot complete your vetting process through other means, what questions would you consider "off limits" during an employment interview?

2) After years of downsizing, outsourcing and offshore production, U.S. corporations are generating increased (some say huge) profits. Has the environment for bloated corporate excess returned?

3) If non-founding CEO's of public corporations are paid a thousand times the average compensation of its employees, are they not pillaging their employers?

4) What life-long lessons did you learn from the temporary jobs you held through high school or college, and how did you apply those lessons in career employment?

Chapter 7

Being of Sound Body and Mind

Frankly, I cannot remember any time when he was sick. He was always healthy. Maybe he suffered an occasional cold or the flu, but nothing worse. Health was a keystone to his long life. He did not exercise; really, nobody from his generation did. He did not see a doctor for regular checkups. Why bother, since he always felt fine? He did not drink, not much at least, and we all ate quite well. He probably regretted not having his eyes regularly checked because the doctors may have caught and minimized the acute cye disease which he developed and that eventually curtailed much of his reading and driving activities in the last fifteen years of his life. Even through adversity he remained optimistic of his future and that of his family.

It may not be the most effective cardiovascular activity, but he was always working outdoors, around the farm in Connecticut or at our home in New Jersey: hauling brush, tree cutting, transplanting, repairing, painting or mowing the grass was his exercise. His most serious ailment or injury that I recall was the one sustained during his unannounced visit to my grandparents' friend, Jon Pol, at his small junkyard down the road. Unfortunately, Mr. Pol had forgotten to close the gate securing the Doberman pinscher that protected the neat piles of discarded treasures. I wasn't there at the junkyard that day. I was back at the farm, but the story goes that when he saw the dog charging at him, he turned quickly to jump back into our Rambler wagon, but the dog was quicker and bit his backside. I never saw the wound, but he enjoyed a full recovery, I was told.

Knowing that all future executives in this highly competitive business world will be challenged more than ever before, I would expect them to be sound in body and mind; that's my axiom for preparedness. If executive management can demonstrate that they are **C**reative, **O**rganized, **R**espectful, **P**repared, **R**esponsible, **E**ducated, **F**it, **O**ptimistic, **R**ational, **M**oral, **E**motionally Stable, **R**esilient and possessing **S**ubstance (**CORP REFORMERS**) then the company should be much more capable of meeting extreme challenges. These challenges will originate from suppliers, clients, customers, competitors, government and other regulatory agencies. After a while, when you think that you have seen and met them all, there is a unique heart-stopping challenge that will require an immediate, measured, equipotent strategic response. I always considered myself reasonably prepared and was put to the test early and often in my business life.

I received a telephone call late one afternoon from a clerk at the local courthouse informing me that Sal Damone, the co-founder of WAC, had filed a "cease-and-desist" order against BORDICO, my own newly founded company. I was further informed that there would be a hearing before a judge the very next day. The plaintiff claimed that I had a non-compete agreement with WAC that prohibited me from engaging in similar business activities. The clerk recommended that I have my attorney present.

Because of the short time between being informed and the court appearance, and with the full knowledge that a non-compete agreement did not exist, I showed up alone, as president and founder of BORDICO, to refute the claim. The most stressful part of it was anticipating the direction that events could take, but I was never intimidated at any time. When it was my turn to speak before the judge I took a deep breath, stood my ground and succinctly defended my position. These are the kinds of situations that you will face at all levels of business, whether or not your disputes are aired in a courtroom. I won that courtroom argument and the judge gave both parties sixty days to settle any remaining disputes, which we did.

Much later, as director of SCAI, I wrote, negotiated and executed contracts for chemicals from numerous foreign suppliers. Moon Chemical Co, Ltd was our Korean chemicals contract supplier with which I had done business for years, despite the fact that they periodically experienced financial instability. It was not so unusual a circumstance when I received a meeting request at my New York office from their new vice president of sales, Mr. Gun-woo Park. I had never met Mr. Park so I was looking forward to the visit. We made the necessary greeting preparations for Mr. Park and two others accompanying him. Since they were also directly involved in this business, I invited three of my own staff to join us for a welcoming lunch. There was nothing unusual about this meeting as I expected it to be mostly a meet-and-greet; that assumption was short lived.

No sooner did our initial conference room gathering get underway than Mr. Park started making demands regarding the most irrelevant things; when we would have lunch, where we would have lunch and his newly announced expectation that I should arrange and travel with him to meet all of my company's major customers using the product in which we formulated Moon's chemical. Though his misguided lecture was absolutely inappropriate, I let the rant go on for just a few minutes more because I wanted to show some modicum of respect for his position; but now it was my turn!

As Mr. Park paused before continuing, I rose from my seat at the conference table and in a calm voice asked everyone except Mr. Park to leave the room for a few minutes. Although my peculiar request was certainly uncharacteristic of me, I felt it was absolutely necessary because I needed to fend off the verbal assault Mr. Park was waging on my staff and determine his motivation. When the room cleared, I asked him to explain why he chose to complain about everything in our first thirty minutes together, and then I asked him what he really wanted.

His demeanor immediately changed, the bluster disappeared and his weaknesses were revealed. I now had to listen to a whining apology in which he explained that he was "under tremendous pressure from [his] new owners to increase [their] contract price by 12%, effective immediately." Although his voice was now meek, it was clear that he had been ordered to announce a unilateral change to our existing contract. The contract which his predecessor and I had negotiated was what we call a "firm-fixed agreement" with a non-changeable contract price for a specified quantity, over a specified time period, at specified payment terms, all of which we had mutually agreed to in writing, with dual authorized signatures. There is no easy way to settle contract disputes when conducting international business. Typically, international business contracts include that ceremonious clause naming the country, city and court branch where disputes would be settled, but most of us understand that enforcement, claim settlement and collection is nearly impossible.

The Koreans' mandated price increase was a potential disaster because my company's pricing to our customers was based on our contracted raw material costs; even small changes would affect our profitability, including a potential loss since there was virtually no opportunity for me to raise prices or cancel our own U.S. customer contracts. I told Mr. Park that I understood his position and told him that I would do all possible to find a mutual solution. After more of Mr. Park's whining, I understood further that unless I agreed to the higher price, they would not make any more shipments, which was even more unacceptable to me and our customers who depended on regular shipments from us.

Unlike my querulous visitor, who had a near mental breakdown in our conference room, I was suitably prepared to understand the consequences of the intolerable terms being imposed on my company and how to respond. Having heard all that I needed, I summoned the others to return to the conference room and we had our lunch brought in, a change from our original dining reservation.

The next day we spent going over some technical and supply chain management details from our original agenda. Then I arranged for Mr. Park and me, along with his staff and one of my own, to visit with several select customers during the balance of the week. The five of us drove to the airport, but upon arrival at the ticket counter, about an hour before our flight, I informed Mr. Park that I had a customer emergency and was being called back to the office. I further announced that my associate, Laura Dinton, who had seen his conference room outburst and was there with us at the airport, would be his host for the balance of the week!

My sole purpose for returning to the office was to begin an immediate, four-month, international, full-court press to identify, test, qualify and replace our contract-breaking supplier with other producers. The three handpicked customers that I sent Mr. Park and the delegation to visit were our smallest—not largest, as he requested—so as to minimize the impending damage from his visit. Not only did I believe that Mr. Park lacked preparedness but was a failure at his attempt to deceive SCAI further. It had crossed my mind (and it was later confirmed) that he sought to enter the U.S. market directly after gaining some customer experience through this first visit, as well as subsequent ones. I did not always catch it early, but I was always aware of the possibility for these kinds of surreptitious, executive business strategies or, as some would call it, the game within the game. It takes a nimble response, some agility and perennial preparedness to catch it early and often.

I saw Gun-woo Park about six months later when he and the new Moon Chemical CEO visited our office once more. This time he was there to complain to SCAI's president, Japanese expatriate Ken Kimura, that I had abruptly replaced 100% of their previous supply. Park informed us that we had been their largest customer and that the financial health of their company now rested on our reinstating their supply. When Mr. Kimura asked why Moon Chemical broke the contract, the miscreant Mr. Park replied, "Because we didn't think that he [me] could replace us." Indeed we did, but these kinds of tireless accomplishments are not for the weak of body or mind.

During my ten years at SCAI, I reported to three consecutive expatriate presidents. It was rare, except in one case, when any of these presidents chose to collaborate on a project with me directly. They seemed to prefer working with the other Japanese expatriates in the U.S. office, call it what you wish.

It's hard to forget my third SCAI president, Tom Watanabe, who struggled mightily to keep up with the fast business pace and style here in the United States. But for a singular two-month period, he conceded to have weekly project meetings in his office so I could update some of the others on strategy changes and my recommendations to navigate through a particularly challenging business undertaking. I wouldn't have been invited under normal circumstances, but I had the most experience in that business area by far. My reporting and recommendations, which I very carefully conceived and articulated, caused Mr. Watanabe to have regular anxiety attacks, during which he became short of breath, began to perspire heavily, wrung his hands and exclaimed, "Oh my God, oh my God." It wasn't an attractive image to project to me or the others attending the meetings.

In the five years he was stationed with us in our small New York office, Mr. Watanabe never once walked the thirty feet from his office to mine, whether to ask a question, collaborate or invite me to lunch to discuss new business development (my specialty). Since he seemed to lack any clear corporate vision himself, I would have been happy to discuss broader business opportunities with him. In fairness to the man, he was essentially ordered and assigned by Tokyo headquarters to our important, revenue-producing New York office. Tokyo never considered whether he was prepared to manage our multiple business units in New York. Instead, they simply followed a longstanding corporate seniority entitlement program. Any C. SATOCHI Corp expatriate stationed in our New York office would receive a financial windfall through SATOCHI's inflated expatriate compensation, which was about double what a U.S. national would earn holding an equivalent position at SCAI. Of course Tom Watanabe agreed to the assignment—he had to and wanted to! In the end, that was unfortunate for all of us because he was not prepared for the arduous tasks associated with the position he occupied. At the very least, in the absence of being fit or prepared, SCAI would have been better served if Mr. Watanabe had remained alert, delegated responsibility and never revealed that he was crumbling inside.

My general disappointment with the lack of executive preparedness in the workplace was recurrent but was exacerbated in one case by a sizable example of nepotism in a large public corporation. It began when the president of Esco White, Tim Warbuck, announced that he was transferring an employee from our Brussels division to the United States to fill a vacancy: vice president of sales and marketing. Tim had been president of the division for many years and maintained his position during the sale by U.S. Ammonium to Esco Oy. The recently retired U.S. Ammonium vice president of research and development, Brian Johnson II, a longtime business colleague and personal friend of Tom, had a son who was still working for U.S. Ammonium, but in a different division. Because Tim and Brian had been friends for such a long time, it was Tim who was the godfather of Brian's oldest son, Brian (John) Johnson III. Under a huge cloud of secrecy, the previously unnamed individual in Brussels who was being transferred to our Savannah, Georgia, office was none other than John Johnson!

Because Tim would not allow competitive interviews for the vacancy and ignored all other protocol for vetting and hiring, he created significant animosity among the mid-level managers and sales representatives. Sometimes, though, you can be pleasantly surprised, so a few of us deferred passing judgment and waited for John Johnson's long anticipated arrival. Within months, Esco White President Tim Warbuck retired, but we all agreed he made a highly subjective and suspect hiring decision, leaving the company with some potential cleanup work to do.

Soon after he established himself at the Savannah office, I took John for an introductory visit to a significant and highly polished client professional. But I was embarrassed when, during the entire hour-long meeting in the client's cavernous, well-appointed office, my boss picked at his fingernails as we sat on the

85

comfortable, overstuffed couches. Fortunately, John Johnson left most of the talking to the client and me, so I was able to distract the client from John's ill-timed manicure. Unfortunately, time proved that John was out of his league as the new VP of sales and marketing, and the thought of his being brought to the United States as a result of the plan that Brian and Tim concocted was repugnant. That sentiment lingered among many of us for years.

Some of the younger, less experienced employees I've worked with knew the basics of their field of study but they sometimes needed a small amount of guidance in preparedness. Take the case of my younger assistant, Laura Dinton, who worked hard at her job in my SCAI department for several years; she took no unexcused absences and was always on time, very smart, quick to complete difficult assignments, promotable and always pleasant to coworkers. Then the day came when the world seemed to crash down on her.

It was outrageous. While I was out of the office on business travel, Yoshiro (Yoshi) Miyake, a less experienced man who worked in another department at the same rank as Laura, was quickly and rather secretly promoted by the "Oh-my-God" president, Tom Watanabe. Yoshi now held a position above Laura in my department. As department manager, I should have been consulted or at the very least informed in advance. Laura and I were both stunned by this obfuscation of protocol. Laura was especially devastated because she had hoped to be rewarded with a promotion if a new position was created in our rapidly growing department; indeed, she deserved it. When I returned to the office the day after the errant promotion was announced, Laura walked into my office and began to cry.

No one but me could have seen her deteriorating condition because she was sitting in a chair on the other side of my desk with her back to the wall-length viewing window. We spoke about the egregious action against us and especially her, but then I had to tell her, "Please don't ever cry in this office again. If the other managers [primarily Japanese expatriates] were to see your current state of mind, they would consider you unfit for promotion and it would be unlikely that you could change their opinion." She had to hear this, and I'm glad she heard it from me. I had a meeting to rush to, so I asked her to remain in my office until she composed herself; keeping one's emotions in check is a part of preparedness.

Unfortunately, due to her mistreatment by Mr. Watanabe, she left the company shortly thereafter, and it took a while for Yoshi Miyake and our entire department to make up for the loss of the highly proficient Laura Dinton. I expected Laura to sue SCAI, because to me, it was a clear case of discrimination when a less qualified employee, a man of SCAI's preferred nationality, was bumped above her in the promotion. She never did sue, but probably should have; sometimes, that's what's needed to change a dysfunctional corporate culture.

If executive preparedness functioning at the highest level, there won't likely be opportunities lost by discarding the treasures that may lead others to financial wealth. These discarded treasures may be product lines that hold little promise of future profits, in the minds of executive management, patents or licenses that appear to hold no immediate value or highly competent employees who fail to gain recognition for their valuable contributions.

An enormous opportunity was lost when Eastman Kodak Company, a recognized market leader mostly known for its film and Brownie cameras, shelved numerous patents for digital imaging, including the fundamental technology for future digital cameras, in favor of protecting their sizable market position in film. At the time of this writing, Kodak is in bankruptcy and is selling off its patents (said to be worth $2 billion), trying to recoup some of the bondholders' stake and attempting to re-invent itself.

It's well-known that arguably the first telecommunications giant in the United States rejected Alexander Graham Bell's offer to sell his newly patented telephone rights. Western Union Telegraph Company simply felt that it was a gadget and preferred to stick with its telegraphic method of communication. The company discontinued those operations in the late twentieth century while sliding in and out of bankruptcies and buyouts.

I've seen many new managers and presidents arbitrarily target competent employees for dismissal. The reasons are not always apparent, but perhaps their own insecurity and weakness made them feel threatened. I recall my first encounter with Ken Kimura after he was transferred from our Tokyo headquarters to become SCAI's president. On his first day in the office he requested all employees to gather in the large conference room for a quick meet-and-greet. After a short speech and a few pleasantries, he targeted one of our senior managers, Jules Steinberg, a PhD in organic chemistry, and ordered him to "tidy up your office, put everything where it belongs and you have a week to do it." Dr. Steinberg may have had a sloppy office, but more serious than that, our new president demonstrated that he himself was sloppy in his thinking. The harassing and demeaning tone continued for another year or so until Jules was demoted and summarily fired without cause. I was promoted to his vacant position but I felt that a company treasure had been needlessly discarded.

Discovery 7

1) *When did your own preparedness prevent a disaster from occurring in your business or personal life?*

2) *What was the most significant Moon Chemical strategy failure?*

3) *In a multi-national company, how do you weigh the benefits gained from appointing expatriate executives against their possible misinterpretation of local business custom, protocol, law or nuance?*

4) *What corporate measures could you take to reduce lost opportunities from patents, licenses or human resources?*

Chapter 8

In Search of Balance:
Family, Work and Friends

As infrequently as they occurred, I always got a kick out the parties that my parents had in the basement of our Ridgewood home. Even if you never visited our home in the early sixties, you may be able to imagine the popular middle-class design from that particular era. The walls were finished with varnished wood paneling having randomly spaced vertical grooves to imitate individual boards. The ceiling, all of seven feet high, was white perforated acoustical tile squares and the floor was covered with variegated brown and tan asphalt tiles intended to give the appearance of cork. There was no bar. He never made that a priority construction project, but then again, he was not a big drinker, nor did he promote it to others.

I recall one party in particular, at Halloween; I must have been around thirteen years old at the time. I learned through general conversation around the house which neighborhood couples were coming (the usual ones), and I thought it hilarious that their middle-aged guests would arrive dressed in costumes. I was home the night of that party, but I was definitely planning on staying out of their way. Just as the fragrance of lilacs or the sound of gentle waves may remind you of a happy place from your past, I still recall that night whenever I hear muffled rhythmic bass resembling the incessant pounding coming from their new Macy's 300-watt stereo speakers.

Through the evening I couldn't even identify the songs being played because the bass was set way too high and the closed doors muffled the sound before it reached my room on the second floor. It could have been some of Herb Alpert's Tijuana Brass playing, one of my parents' favorites at the time.

My curiosity about the entire celebration became so intense that I crept downstairs and made my way to the basement under some pretense so I could see this unimaginable spectacle. I was right. Their friends were dressed as cowgirls, pirates, GI's and such, bobbing for apples and generally carrying on. Bobbing for apples was no longer just a kid's game. These were their friends, making their own fun and genuinely enjoying each other's company. I'm glad I saw that.

This was part of his balanced life, the weighted posture that he sought and held. He seemed to know early on that a certain idyllic balance between family, work and friends (pretty much in that order) was essential to achieving greater happiness in life. Because he expected an early demise, he believed it would be too late for him to pursue a balanced life in a hypothetical retirement that he might never live to see.

At one point in my career I had the sudden revelation that my close business colleagues and I were no longer having fun while performing our jobs. Maybe the others were having fun, but it sure did not appear that way to me. As I saw it, the grinding daily regimen of producing sales and profits had drained us of our emotional connection to both our surroundings and each other.

It felt like it had been forever since I was reveling in an impromptu road trip from Hull, UK to Liverpool with Paul Marsden and a few other business colleagues from Seagull Colours Ltd, a supplier to TOD. We set out that weekend to see a football match between Liverpool and Manchester, but the trip became much more memorable for the many pub visits on the long drive to the stadium in Liverpool, the 0-0 score, Gerry and the Pacemakers' music blasting on the stadium loudspeakers and the nearby River Mersey, from which the name of the Pacemakers' endearing trademark song was derived, *Ferry Cross the Mersey*.[4] On another weekend layover in the UK, in another year, I found it fascinating to walk through York to see the Roman ruins two millennia old. This time my host was Seagull's Stewart Cox, and his family too! When on business travel, making the time to engage in non-business activities was an extremely rare occurrence for me.

But closer to home, on that very day of my revelation, I was driving to visit customers in upstate New York and was accompanied by my Esco White manager, Dr. Hyde. I'm not sure what compelled me on that specific day, but I didn't feel that I was taking any risks by confiding my impression that none of us were having fun at our jobs any longer. I went on to suggest that we should compel ourselves to find opportunities in our work to enjoy the cities we visit, the customers with whom we conduct business and especially those within our own company. After considering my recommendation and knowing our limited opportunities to make changes, he decided—with my full consent—to spend the rest of the afternoon after our customer appointments visiting his alma mater!

As Dr. Hyde knew, we were only a few minutes away from his alma mater, State University of New York (SUNY)- Albany. Because it was the first day of spring, he explained that it was tradition for SUNY students to climb into the large courtyard fountain to celebrate the onset of warmer weather and the approaching end of the academic year. We were just in time to see that annual ritual conclude; then we walked into the science building so he could seek out a professor who he said was a large influence on his PhD dissertation.

Once he found the professor, I could see how much he enjoyed reminiscing about the time they shared together more than fifteen years earlier. After leaving the campus, Dr. Hyde was anxious to have me drive past some of his old haunts in Albany and to see how much things had changed since his departure. This proved to be a lot of fun for him, and I enjoyed the short break from the business routine, too. We agreed we would report back to each other, perhaps monthly, to share what work-related fun we had created.

You may already sense the outcome of our innocuous pact; after that day, a mere twelve hours later, we lapsed back into the disciplined business methodology that had made us successful managers: focus, technical knowledge, professionalism and customer service. Even though I was the one who had suggested more fun, I rarely allowed for any personal time during business trips. Yet an entire year later, while traveling on business for Lumitech, I turned half a day's dead time between Los Angeles customer visits into an opportunity to visit the LaBrea Tar Pits. It turned out to be another fascinating and thoroughly enjoyable jaunt; sadly, because Dr. Hyde and I were no longer working together, he never learned of my effort.

I did better in the decades afterwards, forcing myself to schedule a closer inspection of my unique business surroundings. After one of my business meetings with Gavin and Tong, my Chinese suppliers, we all jumped into their car and made a memorable impromptu trip to Shaoshan, Mao's childhood country home. Other opportunities for personal enlightenment followed, like my strategy planning dinners at Tokyo Yakitori (skewered chicken) with Yamamoto and Hashimoto, my productive and entertaining Japan-based colleagues. Chemical sourcing trips to India occasionally took me to the coast of the Arabian Sea from Mumbai to Trivandrum. Accompanied by Madhav, my business colleague and friend, we frequently stopped to get some fresh cashews at the local markets or visit one of the many ancient temples. I made less historical visits to karaoke in Korea with DW Kim, my friend and business agent, and I will never forget the last time I met up with Ken Arai and some other Japanese colleagues at one of Tokyo's late night karaoke clubs, which concluded with all of us singing the most offensive chorus to John Denver's *Country Roads*. It was beautiful!

Not everyone understands the limits of fun at work; I cite the odd predilection of Todd Reynolds, U.S. Ammonium's perennial national sales manager. During the course of his business travel, he spent a great deal of the company's time and money on coast-to-coast golf junkets. He was a likable guy and was said to have a ten handicap; employees would say that he was on the PGA tour. I think that he carried fun to an extreme. Whenever he could, he would ask a customer or industry colleague to accompany him for a round of golf, but the invitations were mostly intended to make these outings more palatable to the company accountants who would approve his expense reports for reimbursement.

It's also said that he played over three hundred golf courses while he crisscrossed the country on business travel. Amazing! My issue here is twofold. Did Todd waste valuable company time, for which he was paid a substantial salary, to satisfy his personal needs? And if so, why should the company feel obligated to pay for any of it?

Just as I'd done at NICO Metals, one of the duties of my SCAI job was to review salespeople's expense reports. Increasingly, I had to draw lines between what I considered business entertainment and something other than that; sometimes *way* beyond that. Some of this business entertainment was so outrageously expensive and unrelated that it annoyed me to imagine that anyone would think it was appropriate and it was even more annoying that anyone would think I would approve the expense for reimbursement. In all the improbable cases presented to me at SCAI, I would bring the expense report for further review to the current expatriate president; for a time, that was Mr. Watanabe. I would begin by stating that I refused to approve it, but if he wanted to, he could, of course.

For the most part, the SCAI salespeople and managers who continuously tested the company's tolerance provided very little evidence to corroborate their expense reports. For example, I would be provided with a nondescript receipt for an $800 dinner for three, none of whom were customers or suppliers. In most large conventional companies, operating manuals clearly define which employee travel and entertainment expenses will be reimbursed. The rules typically set forth certain minimum requirements that the entertainment expenses 1) relate to a business purpose, 2) pertain to legitimate customers, prospects or suppliers and 3) can be documented with a descriptive receipt. One hundred percent of the time, Mr. Watanabe would reverse my decision and approve the expense report I rejected. For a permanent record, I always asked,

"How could our three salespeople spend that kind of money for dinner?" What always followed was the same answer for that category of expense: "It's an after-hours Japanese piano bar; it's okay, Jeff san." I suppose Mr. Watanabe thought I understood; I did—I understood it as a flagrant misuse of company funds!

But there are lots of other ways to have fun and experience new things during business travel at no cost to you or the company. I had been visiting various western Massachusetts customers for years and sometimes stayed overnight at one of the national hotel chain brands. Because I was going to be traveling there, this time with Esco White's Raines McGowan, I asked him to reserve hotel rooms for the both of us. I was sure this was fine because he had also visited the area many times before, but never with me. Instead of the hotel experience that I was accustomed to, he booked us at The Red Lion Inn, Stockbridge, Massachusetts, for an equal or lower daily rate than what I had recently paid elsewhere.

The difference in the experience? Nightly entertainment in one of the few New England hotels that has been under continuous operation since the eighteenth century, an excellent restaurant and comfortable, period-decorated rooms; no two are alike. During our stay, I made time to linger on the sprawling front porch, savoring the evening streetscape from one of the inn's many rocking chairs. Bucolic Stockbridge street scenes like this were a favorite subject for America's beloved twentieth-century American illustrator, painter and Stockbridge resident, Norman Rockwell (1894-1978). After that first stay at this marvelous hotel, I have not stayed anywhere else when in the area for business or pleasure.

I would call it more reflective and thoughtful than fun, but on another one of my business weekend layovers, being without any traveling companion this time, I took the Shinkansen (bullet train) from Tokyo to Kyoto. Upon arrival, I tried looking beyond the main streets to imagine a former time when the teahouse and the art of the geisha were a way of life. Prior to that business trip to Japan, I had read Arthur Golden's masterful story, *Memoirs of a*

Geisha. This was not such an unusual precursor for me because I often sought recommendations for other books that explored the culture or history of the business destinations I visited. That particular novel was recommended to me by the always surefooted Ms. Tezuka, one of my coworkers, Japanese-born and New York University educated. The book was fascinating and enhanced my cultural understanding and I recommend that you also seek a deeper understanding of business culture, particularly if you have an international responsibility.

Yes, work is work. You are principally contributing to the objectives of the organization by meeting the goals assigned. Because work should inherently provide some degree of personal satisfaction, wouldn't it be best if you were engaged in work activity that you enjoy? If you're engaged to a lesser degree, you may have found the examples of my personal experience useful in creating more satisfaction and enjoyment through work. Yet work is only one aspect of being a balanced person. The other significant components are family and friends. There are still other components, but perhaps they are less significant to balance. Because I believe that all of us are drawn to family, work and friends as part of the human condition, it also follows that there should be balance. Keep in mind that family, work and friends can be broadly defined. Family, for example, can include those emotionally close to us; work can mean the act of being industrious anywhere, including the home, your place of worship or where you volunteer, and friends can mean anything you want it to mean, including all those hundreds of Facebook friends.

It's rare to come across executive managers who have balance in their lives. I really don't know why. Dr. Hyde, however, was someone who did! During the few years that we worked together at Esco White, I saw his work ethic and performance up close, met his family and understood what they meant to him. Because he made himself accessible and maintained a positive attitude throughout it all, he attracted friends wherever he went. Esco

White was eventually sold and he went on to become a VP at minerals producer Omya, Inc. Dr. Hyde was a good teacher and friend and most certainly a balanced man.

Long before I was introduced to Dr. Hyde I was a coworker of Dr. Planck, a NICO Metals vice president. He had a broad understanding of metallurgy and much more; he probably blasted a 300-watt stereo at home and had more fun in his basement, living room or any other room than you could imagine. He was a continuous stream of consciousness, conversant on practically any subject and his jovial demeanor made him a great travel companion. Our local business trips together gave us ample opportunities to discuss random subjects in a rather open-ended dialogue that sometimes pushed the realm of normal cerebration. He claimed to be the great grandson of Max Planck, the German physicist, Nobel Prize winner and arguably the founder of Quantum Theory. I don't even know if his ancestral claim was true but it certainly added to his mystique. I recall that Dr. Planck even claimed to be an MD.

It was not unusual for the two of us to make joint visits to customers and then drive back to the office together to pick up the other's car, sometimes as late as 10:00 p.m. Although I wasn't even thirty years old at the time, I would usually be mentally and physically exhausted from one of the grueling joint calls with Dr. Planck, who was probably twenty-five years my senior. Upon one of our return trips, he declared that we should go into the city, meaning New York City, because he knew a great Chinese restaurant there. Although it was now after 10:00 p.m. and we were probably an hour away from the restaurant, I didn't let my fatigue derail Dr. Planck's idea. I really felt like heading home but I simply could not pass up on this marvelous opportunity to enjoy some camaraderie with one of my most esteemed colleagues. Throughout the dinner we discussed everything but business. We were friends, having a fun night and genuinely enjoying each other's company. Dr. Planck was a balanced man indeed!

Now here's a different scenario: not too long ago, on another long car ride to visit customers, my boss, Ajeet Malik from Ajeet Chemicals, lamented that while he knew a great deal about our products, our markets and customers, he was unable to discuss other far-ranging topics that I broached to pass the time. I don't believe his revelation was intended as a compliment to me as much as an acknowledgement of his shortcomings in being a balanced man, or even caring to be a balanced man. In fairness, he had a mind born to serve the chemicals industry.

There are two other men whom I'm compelled to mention in this book. One is Lawrence Kabala, my friend and coworker at TOD and the other is Ron Nightingale, a close neighborhood friend who coincidentally worked in the chemicals industry, at Chemic Corporation, a global chemicals company. Both men had great jobs, were highly intelligent and were very well organized, even perfectionists. It's easy to compare them because they shared so many wonderful traits, the kind you would seek out and value among your staff and new hires.

A simplified priority for a weighted balance between family, work and friends was created in this chapter. Both Lawrence and Ron lost balance somewhere along the way. I do believe that my two friends let their work overwhelm them, prioritizing it above all else, and when circumstances at work, things beyond their control, adversely skewed their perception of their own performance, there was a catastrophic end. Unfortunately, both men, believing there was no other course of action, took their own lives a few years apart. I miss them both and mention them here to honor them and to cite them as a stark and reverent reminder of the significance of balance. No one should ever feel that things are flying that far out of control at work; stay balanced, enough said.

Your view of the bigger world around you, beyond family, work and friends, to include balance with faith, volunteerism and philanthropy, is part of who you are. Enjoy the experience, it is a gift.

Discovery 8

1) *What would you consider the limit to reasonable fun during business hours, and what do you consider reasonable reimbursable business entertainment?*

2) *When is your next opportunity to incorporate an enjoyable diverting experience through work? What will it be?*

3) *Have you ever read a book, fiction or non-fiction, describing some aspect of a culture other than your own?*

4) *Would you consider your own life balanced?*

Chapter 9

Building Your Own Legacy

When you live as long as he did, you have heard the stories probably a hundred times, or at least it feels that way. Nevertheless, I would still love to hear them a hundred more times in my own life. During WWII, he was called to serve in the Army and after basic training was sent to Panama to guard the canal against attack. As a key troop and supply passage from the Pacific to the Atlantic, control was essential to the United States. By the grace of God, the canal was never attacked, although after the war, secret plans to invade the canal area were discovered. That's the history and the rest might be historical fiction. Who really knows?

But during his four years of duty in Panama he became fluent in Spanish, slowed his pace from the tropical heat and adopted some native pets. As the story goes, upon awakening one morning, he discovered that his pet monkey had disappeared, but his macaw remained. Because monkeys were a regular part of the locals' diet, it was widely presumed that the monkey had become some family's dinner!

Later, I was always glad to hear how he and the other G.I.'s enjoyed swimming in Panama's ocean surf. Of course I would never have joined them after hearing that their safety was assured only by the degree of accuracy of the sharpshooter designated to sit on the adjacent dunes to keep a watchful eye for sharks.

From a totally different dimension of his experience, he would tell us about his brief amateur career in vaudeville theater, probably in the early 1930's. For some reason, he would always seem to reminisce about that experience when we were traveling from the farm back to our New Jersey home, usually later at night, and seemingly on the same stretch of road. He would conclude by singing one of the old verses softly and slowly, and then he would pick up the tempo and volume until he was booming the chorus until he was done. It was a song about working peoples' struggles prior to the French Revolution, and I still remember some of the words; *"Sons of toil and danger, will you serve a stranger, and bow down to Burgundy. Onward! Onward! Swords against the foe. Forward! Forward the lily banners go!*"[5] He sang it with passion, as though he was proclaiming his own freedom; but from what, from whom? He had a very good voice, really, but rarely sang other than during the circumstance that I described. Too bad, I would have enjoyed hearing more of it.

What is the relevance of how you may be remembered after you have left the military, organization or company? After all, you may say, "it's just work." Your legacy is measured by the impact that you had on others working alongside you in pursuing common objectives, then remembered later by those who remained, not only as a source of a warm and fuzzy moment for them, but more significantly, as a basis for enhancing workplace culture. Your workplace legacy to be measured is the sum of your accomplishments: what you created, the trust you shared, how you led, your preparedness and how you established an enjoyable environment for others who contributed to the common cause.

It is far better to hear others say, "How brilliant she was," "How he saved the company," "He was the best salesman ever born" or "She always had a smile on her face" than to work for a lifetime and virtually go unnoticed, like you never were even there. I absolutely love hearing a former coworker telling stories about me and Lawrence Kabala working together at TOD, calling us the "go to guys" when there was a problem with no apparent desirable solution. Although I don't remember it exactly that way and certainly never heard it from my boss at the time, I still consider it part of my work legacy.

The legacy of Steve Jobs as co-founder of Apple Inc, the highly successful international consumer electronics, software and computer design company, is truly remarkable, but also remarkable to me was the legacy of Jerry Morrison, Davis & Elkins College mailroom clerk. During my four years at college, I never saw Jerry sitting down, frowning or complaining. Instead, he was always moving in high gear, efficiently going about his job with a pleasant way of accommodating all of us students with kind words and a smile. It was no surprise when our college yearbook was dedicated to Jerry, ahead of the college dean and president. We may not have known Steve Jobs personally, but we all personally know someone like Mr. Morrison, who is still remembered forty years later. Now that is legacy!

Beyond the workplace, *Live* is also about the broader legacy that you leave behind for family and friends. From that perspective, the impact of your own legacy on your generational family is likely to be exponentially greater than your legacy from workplace contributions. It is indisputable that Steve Jobs created groundbreaking consumer products, related employment and spectacular stock investment results, but few of us will have the capability to replicate that level of contribution. Instead, most of our own lives will be enriched by the satisfaction of knowing that we might have rendered non-financial treasures—values, ethics and good judgment—to family and even friends.

And what about the monkey and the macaw? Was it just a G.I.'s story or was it another metaphor of some natural order that we have no control over, at work or anywhere else? The macaw survived, but why? Certainly his flight-from-risk ability was an advantage over the ground-based monkey. Or maybe the monkey was too trusting and was too easily enticed by others with a false promise of food or something else, just moments before his capture and demise.

And maybe there is very little difference between the sharks and sharpshooters in the story. You would expect that after surviving hundreds of millions of years of evolution, the shark's instincts would affirm its safety as the apex predator. However, it would have no capacity to anticipate the invisible threat beyond its natural boundaries. Although I'm going to believe that the sharpshooter's purpose was merely defensive, I've encountered many difficult-to-identify predatory threats within and outside normal workplace boundaries. Whether I considered myself a monkey, macaw, shark or sharpshooter at any given time, I always believed that I was vulnerable!

Since most of the circumstances described in this book, the colorful and nondescript people I met and the predictable and sometimes unexpected outcome of their interactions involved me directly, they are now my own personal stories, just like the monkey and macaw, sharpshooters, sharks and vaudeville were his. So, boom your own chorus occasionally, it will be good for your spirit and will further define for others who you are. Although the positive impact you have on others may be undetectable by you at the time, never be afraid to sing out among others surrounding you at work or elsewhere.

Discovery 9

1) *Why does it matter what kind of employee you become? Will you be the one who made a lasting contribution or one who went largely unnoticed?*

2) *Do you feel you are too trusting? If so, what precautions can you take to survive in a business environment?*

3) *You may feel that you are currently at a personal apex, but seriously, what are some obscure external threats facing you over the next few years?*

4) *Employment is not a vaudeville stage and there is a downside in letting your coworkers share in more of your life than appropriate. What limits do you want to set and what is the downside if you go beyond those limits?*

Chapter 10

Few Things are Accomplished Alone

William Gaius Krizan breathed his last breath at 10:05 a.m., September 11, 2008. I am grateful and comforted by the knowledge that in my fifty-six years with him I said all of the things I wanted to say, especially during the last six months of his life. Since his passing, the values-shaping memories randomly flash through my mind and are welcomed because they provide me with great happiness as a substitute for the few more months I hoped I could have had with him, to learn more from him. The enigma of his life as a balanced man is clearer now, and in time I expect to understand it more deeply, after I have had more time to reflect on our relationship and his solid values.

For the final Christmas of his life I had written a poem for him, put it in a small blue frame and wrapped it in red Christmas paper as his gift. I never had a chance to give it to him. The day that my wife, my three children and I were driving to visit my parents at their Connecticut home, the same home that my grandparents had lived in, the same home in which I learned so many lessons, he suffered a stroke and was taken by ambulance to the hospital prior to our arrival.

Our Christmas gift exchange plans took a dramatically different course, as he would never return to the family home that he so dearly loved. After a short hospitalization, he was taken directly to a nursing facility to live the rest of his life in peace and surrounded by love. This is the poem that he never saw or heard; my gift was eventually opened by my mother, and she carefully placed it on the living room shelves that he built so many years ago.

"Horn & Hardart"[©6] (The Poem)

Remember when we took it slow, with Grandpa Joe and summers would last forever. We went for walks, always talked and got ice cream from Carvel. When I was nine, dad made wine and grew zucchinis so much larger.

What's the time? Hey you got a dime, but that's not enough for Starbucks. It's much more now, I don't know how, whatever happened to Horn & Hardart?

Mighty Mouse was on the way, to save the day and Popeye loved Olive Oyle. We lost the race, with Yuri in space, but the moon was so much better. We got Green Stamps, went to Boy Scout camps and loved our Rambler wagon.

What's the time? Hey you got a dime, but that's not enough for Starbucks. It's much more now, I don't know how, whatever happened to Horn & Hardart?

50 Cent is king, hybrid the thing, but I still go home for Christmas. You I.M.'d today, sold it on e-Bay, but I still hand-write letters. Sushi's a meal, laptops have appeal, but I'm in a country mood today.

What's the time? Hey you got a dime, but that's not enough for Starbucks. It's much more now, I don't know how, whatever happened to Horn & Hardart?

Our lives have been built upon the backs of many who came before us. It is very easy for me to express my gratitude for the business opportunities I earned through formal education, informal training, hard work and the ones that I simply stepped into. At the time it made sense to me, but today, I cannot specifically explain how my career path choices are all connected, either metaphysically or empirically. What did my paper route have to do with my being named director of a $500 million chemicals division and what future inspiration had I received from landing a sweet job in the kitchen at Camp Nel-K-Mar, a girls summer camp, when I was just sixteen years old? It was, and still is, a very crooked road; nonetheless, I am very grateful for the opportunities and choices.

Mr. Ackerman, the local painting contractor and family friend who hired me to work during my college breaks, is primarily responsible for revealing the simplicity of earning a sustained living through a business you can start yourself and the exhilaration that comes from managing that business. Because he provided a needed service to customers and was fiscally responsible, I saw that you can live in a comfortable house, own a reliable car and pay for your kids' college education. That's the way I began to see my own future; simply put, it was the American Dream of the past generation. As a result, in the fall of my junior year, after spending yet another summer working for Mr. Ackerman, I had a final epiphany, realized the American Dream was a real opportunity for me and changed my major from physical education to business.

Never in my life did I measure my own success or that of others by income alone. During those summers painting for Mr. Ackerman, we worked side by side with Joseph Tejas, a man in his forties, born in the United States, of Native American ancestry, who probably never had the opportunity for a full public education. He didn't read or write, and was not very conversant, just quiet; but he was always smiling! Because Joseph could not read maps, street signs or write down basic directions, Mr. Ackerman would drive to meet Joseph early in the morning whenever we were switching job sites. They would meet at some mutually agreed upon location, and my coworker Joseph, in his own car, would follow Mr. Ackerman to the new job site. For years this continued, or as long as those two worked together. That continuous act of kindness, mutual respect and dedication gives you a better understanding of my gratitude to both of them and the measure of true wealth.

In *Live*'s "Making Others Look Good," we discussed the rogue, self-absorbed nature of Porter Benjamin, the retiring executive charged with the responsibility of training me. I have patiently held off until now to describe an entirely different experience that I had from an additional training program a few years later, conducted by another retiring industry legend at TOD. Unlike the former training program, this one was smooth and rewarding! The difference? My new trainer, Roman Evdo, was organized, respectful and focused. But more than anything else, he simply loved to share his formidable knowledge, with me, customers and colleagues alike! He was always more interested in making others look good rather than trying to take the credit for himself. In addition to the scientific and marketing details passed along to me while shadowing him for a few months, I learned much more about the man and how he preferred to interact with his business colleagues and the world around him. After his retirement, Mr. Evdo was missed by all of us. He was one-of-a-kind, and for my experience with him, I am truly grateful.

Well before that, by the time I was twenty-two, I had been given so much by so many that my gratitude far exceeded what I was able to return in kind. During graduate school at West Virginia University, my funds from a prior interim marketing job at Burroughs Corp, a U.S. computer manufacturer, were running low. Fortuitously, I heard some chatter that Gene's Beer Garden, up the street from where I lived, was looking for a bartender.

Before continuing, I have to tell you that Gene's was a small, but successful, family-owned bar. It had been a local gathering place since opening in the mid-forties, and it was owned by the Perilli's: brothers Gene, Joe and Frank and their sister, Katy. They had never hired anybody outside of their family due to trust issues in this cash business. Gene's Beer Garden was on the street level of a two-story, plain, brick, residential neighborhood building, and Gene himself lived in the second floor apartment. A Southern rock-filled jukebox and clickety-clacking pinball machines lined the two walls of the game room toward the back of the main bar area and a narrow hallway led to another room—the barber shop— a room that had not likely changed since the returning WWII vets got their new haircuts. Gene's Beer Garden was primarily known for its friendly atmosphere, serving local regulars beer, chili dogs, Bar-B-Q sandwiches and pickled eggs.

Coincidentally, at that time I was already renting an apartment from Gene's son, which made the entree to an interview a bit easier for me. Without wasting much time, an interview was set up during the bar's off hours. Upon my arrival, Frank directed me to sit in one of the austere, vintage wooden booths and asked that I provide him with details of my background and work experience. Since my previous jobs had been part-time or temporary, I found that he really wasn't interested in the skimpy resume that I had brought with me, nor did he ask for references, which I thought was unusual.

The first question in my interview was, "Have you ever worked in a place like this?" I don't know what I was thinking, exactly, but I responded incredulously, "I have never even seen a place like this!" I guess that was a good answer, and from my response to the other questions, I got the job. As informal as that interview seemed to me at the time, Frank had actually very carefully crafted sequential questions to reveal the level of my work ethic and trustworthiness.

Because the Pirellis became my second family for the two years that I lived in Morgantown, I was always very willing to help with some of their construction, painting or clean-up projects at the numerous properties they owned. It was the least I could do in return for their friendship, but they always insisted that I accept payment for my services. It was at this point in my life that I understood I could no longer exclusively show my gratitude in the conventional ways, with store-bought cards or small gifts that I could purchase. I needed to find a way to return my gratitude in a far more meaningful manner, through substantive actions and deeds! Only a few years ago I had the same overwhelming feeling that I had again accumulated considerably more gratitude than I returned. To remedy that imbalance, I announced to my small volunteer group that I would give 1,000 hours of my time to meritorious non-profit organizations. I fulfilled that promise within two years, but I am still volunteering much of my time to stay somewhat even with my gratitude.

Gene's Beer Garden was sold years ago and Frank is the only surviving original owner. Despite his physical limitations, we still communicate occasionally. But try as I did to return the family's affection, which began in the seventies, my gratitude still far outweighs that which I meant to return to the Perilli family.

My own living room shelves and the walls in my office are now crowded with the blue-framed poem and other pictures and gifts as symbols and physical representations of the gratitude that has uplifted me through the years. Yet no matter where I work or travel, what I may encounter, good or bad, it is the cherished memory of those who provided me with old-fashioned values, insight, logic, compassion and métier that I carefully hold in the forefront of my psyche and which bears predominantly upon my everyday life, including family, work and friends.

Discovery 10

1) *How will you most likely achieve business success, through education, hard work or luck?*

2) *How should you feel when the gifts you receive far outweigh the gifts you give to others?*

3) *How significant a role should the candidate's values play in an employee selection process?*

4) *Which inspiring people or events are you storing on your own shelves or in your subconscious?*

Chapter 11

Future Goals

Indeed, whatever happened to Horn & Hardart? You may have already understood that the poem was a metaphor designed to illuminate similarity to a larger concept. The Horn & Hardart business was the end result of two Americans, Joseph Horn and Frank Hardart, who innovated based on an established fast food restaurant model from Germany. The Horn & Hardart restaurants, some of which were called Automats, provided New York and Philadelphia lunch and dinner patrons with the novelty of simple, low cost, prepared meals. You could view your meal choices through small windows on the rows of individual food storage compartments. The change from your pocket, when inserted into the slot next to your preference, quickly provided you access to your sandwich or dessert.

Joseph Horn and Frank Hardart built their business from the middle of the twentieth century to a solid level of success decades later. Patrons were still enjoying the convenience of the Automats when other fast food restaurants emerged to fill an expanding takeout market. Horn & Hardart was a great success through the forties and fifties and then barely survived into the sixties. But in the seventies, the rapid expansion of national fast food restaurants, which had themselves innovated on an established business model, shoved Horn & Hardart into oblivion within the next decade.

The opportunities and threats to Horn & Hardart restaurants and my father's generation, The Greatest Generation, through the thirties, forties and fifties made them unique. In reality, my father was an everyman, arguably not very different than any family member, friend, classmate or coworker from whom you have already received a positive values-based lesson. However, it's highly unlikely that any of us will ever see the magnitude of values forged by The Greatest Generation or the replication of the once-beloved Horn & Hardart restaurants.

Because of the positive contribution and influence of those who came before us, we have the opportunity to integrate some of their values into our accumulated body of experience and education. This potent combination can be used to create a business environment that improves quality of life and strives for a greater good. It is not only a means, but it is an obligation that I always consider in the important decisions that I make.

In 1926 songwriter Harry M. Woods penned the classic song, *Red, Red Robin,* which was recorded and popularized by the well-known vaudevillian Al Jolson. Coincidentally, thirty years later it was sung by me for a bit part in my kindergarten play. It contained the line; "L*ive, love, laugh and be happy*," which reinforces much of what I learned from my father. And on my own last day on Earth, if given a chance to reflect upon the sum of my life, it is predictable that I will not lament, "I should have worked more." Instead, I am quite certain to say, "I should have lived, loved, laughed and been happy more. My family, work and friends are already testament to my values—that is my legacy." In the years ahead, I will continue to strive to incorporate that personal philosophy into everything I do.

Discovery 11

1)   *What is the "Horn & Hardart" metaphor?*

2)   *What does "Live, love, laugh and be happy" mean to you?*

3)   *Do you agree that all of us have an obligation to improve the quality of life for the greater good?*

4)   *If you knew tomorrow was your last day on Earth and you had to go to work today, what changes would you like to make there?*

Story Pictures

W.G. Krizan with his pet macaw sans monkey
(Panama, 1944)

Kindergarten graduation, St. Emeric's School
(New York City, 1956)

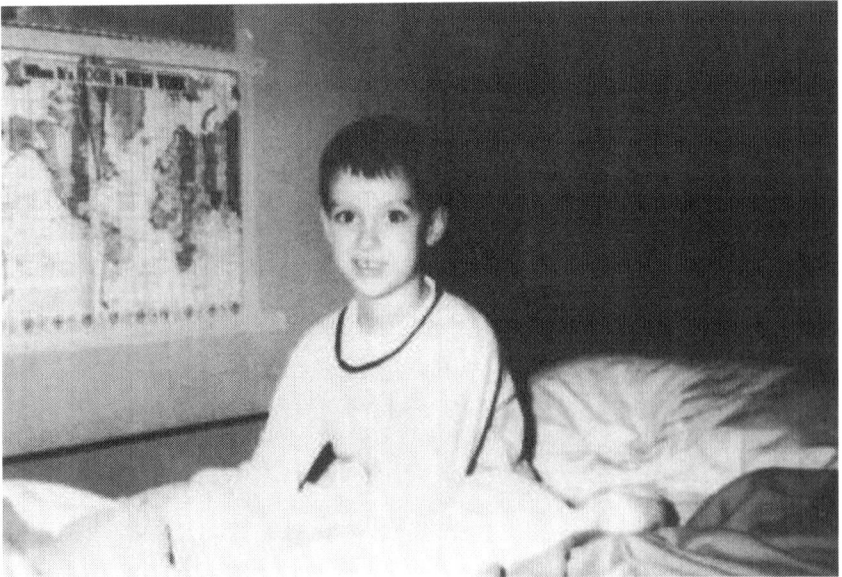

The train town, hinged securely to my bedside wall
(Stuyvesant Town, 1957)

Hatch Pond adventure experience with a crappie in hand
(South Kent, CT, 1959)

Our dog Red following the leader of the pack
(Ridgewood, NJ, 1963)

Bobbing for apples at the Halloween party
(Ridgewood, NJ, 1964)

Our trustworthy Rambler wagon inside the Ridgewood garage
(Ridgewood, NJ, 1964)

Another zucchini-munching woodchuck had his last garden meal
(South Kent, CT, 1966)

Celebrating Fathers' Day
(South Kent, CT, 1985)

Family gathering at the farm
(South Kent, CT, 1993)

W.G. Krizan in his living room fixing his little grandson's toy
(South Kent, CT, 1995)

Revealing the enigma—balance in his everyday life
(At the farm, South Kent, CT, 2007)

Index

Footnotes

[1] Teflon® is a registered trademark of EI DuPont

[2] Post-It-Notes® is a registered trademark of 3M

[3] Qiana® is a registered trademark of EI DuPont

[4] *Ferry Cross the Mersey* (1964), Gerry Marsden

[5] From Song of the Vagabonds, Broadway's- The Vagabond King
(1925), Rudolf Friml/Brian Hooker/W.H. Post

[6] "Horn & Hardart" poem- copyright © JF Krizan, 2006

About the Author

JF Krizan was born in New York City, the son of William G. and Emily B. Krizan. He graduated from Ridgewood High School, Ridgewood, New Jersey, in 1969 and from Davis & Elkins College with a BS in Management in 1973. He attended the MBA program at West Virginia University from 1974-1975. During the next thirty-five years, Mr. Krizan became a most discerning executive through his association with seventeen companies, through conventional employment and by founding or co-founding nine of them.

He knows that his moral challenges and discoveries within those seventeen companies have meaning for any other employee, business owner, business student or curious mind. Mr. Krizan now devotes all of his time to writing and is managing director of Shelter Rock Grant Writing Associates, an organization which he founded in 2011. Mr. Krizan is a Life Member of American Mensa.

"If I didn't believe that business sustainability can be increased through the application of traditional values, that a shift in the current business paradigm is critical to our times and that happiness from living a more balanced life is achievable, *Live* could not have been written."

Made in the USA
Charleston, SC
26 May 2013